M·AGRIPPA·L·F·COS·TERTIVM·FECIT

ROME

POCKET GUIDE

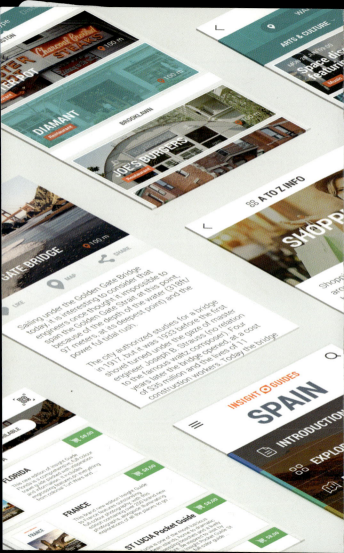

Walking Eye
mobile app

Discover the world's best destinations with the Insight Guides Walking Eye app, available to download for free in the App Store and Google Play.

The container app provides easy access to fantastic free content on events and activities taking place in your current location or chosen destination, with the possibility of booking, as well as the regularly-updated Insight Guides travel blog: Inspire Me. In addition, you can purchase curated, premium destination guides through the app, which feature local highlights, hotel, bar, restaurant and shopping listings, an A to Z of practical information and more. Or purchase and download Insight Guides eBooks straight to your device.

TOP 10 ATTRACTIONS

THE COLOSSEUM
Ancient Rome's spectacular arena.
See page 38.

VILLA BORGHESE PARK
Home to the excellent Galleria Borghese, the Etruscan Museum and a modern art museum. See page 57.

THE TREVI FOUNTAIN
Throw a coin to guarantee your return to Rome. See page 54.

THE SPANISH STEPS
The Eternal City's most popular meeting place. See page 49.

VILLA D'ESTE
One of Italy's greatest gardens. See page 84.

THE SISTINE CHAPEL
The awe-inspiring ceiling by Michelangelo is the highlight. See page 70.

CAMPO DE' FIORI
Rome's colourful open-air market. See page 45.

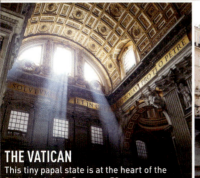

THE ROMAN FORUM
Imposing ruins mark the hub of the ancient city that ruled a vast empire for centuries. See page 31.

THE VATICAN
This tiny papal state is at the heart of the Catholic church. See page 59.

THE PANTHEON
Ancient Rome's best-preserved monument – its ceiling is an amazing feat of engineering. See page 40.

A PERFECT DA

9.00am

Breakfast

Start your day in Trastevere at Caffè delle Arance (Piazza Santa Maria in Trastevere, 2), where along with espresso and *cornettos*, the house special is freshly-squeezed orange juice (served with cubes of ice on the side) and great people-watching right on the piazza.

12.30pm

Cross the Tiber

Cross pedestrian Ponte Sisto and go straight up Vi Pettinari. Turn left on Via dei Giubbonari for great shopping and stop for lunch or snacks right on Campo de Fiori where the city's most picturesque market is still held.

11.30am

Galleries

Head down through Trastevere's winding streets towards Piazza Trilussa and the Tiber, checking out the boutiques and galleries.

10.00am

Janiculum Hill

Take Via Garibaldi to Piazzale Garibaldi at the top of Janiculum Hill for splendid views of the city and the dome of St Peter's. On your way up, veer off towards San Pietro in Montorio church for a peek at Bramante's Tempietto.

1.30pm

Piazza Navona

Cross busy Corso Vittorio Emanuele and take Corso Rinascimento. To the is the sprawling Piazz Navona. Check out Bernini's fountain in t centre and grab a clas if pricey espresso, or better still, the dark chocolate ice cream *tartufo* at bar Tre Scal

nish Steps

east along the narrow Via dei Pastini and follow the ping streets Via del Corso and Via Condotti to Piazza pagna. Give your credit cards a break at the Keats-ley House at the base of the Spanish Steps, and then down Via del Babuino to the sculptor Canova's old io at No.150, which has been transformed into a e with marble masterpieces at every corner.

10.30pm

Trendy bar

Walk up the street for fancy drinks at Doney, which is as posh and popular with today's trendy set as it was at the time of *la dolce vita*.

5pm

theon

e right of Corso sscimento on llel road Via Di S. anna D'Arco, you'll the San Luigi dei cesi church at 5. Inside are three aravaggio's most ous paintings, uding *The Calling of Matthew*. Take Via Seminario and you'll e Pantheon.

5.00pm

Art in the park

Walk through Villa Borghese Park and check out the Carlo Bilotti Modern Art Collection.

7.30pm

Dinner

Catch bus 490 or 495 and get off at the last stop inside the park. Cross under the arch and into Via Veneto. Dine at Chef Claudio Mengoni's Michelin-starred Assaje Restaurant for unforgettable Italian cuisine; book a seat on the patio in good weather.

CONTENTS

INTRODUCTION

'All roads lead to Rome' is not just a figure of speech. In ancient times all routes did indeed radiate from the capital of the Roman Empire. Rome, the Eternal City, was seen as the *caput mundi* – 'capital of the world', ruler of an empire stretching from Gaul and Spain in the west to Egypt and Asia Minor in the east, attracting many different peoples and bequeathing many different legacies to history. But, unlike other comparable cultures that have left a shadow of their former selves, Rome has continued to hold sway.

Not only was it an artistic mecca during the Renaissance, and a sanctuary for well-to-do travellers doing the 'Grand Tour' in the 19th century but, as the centre of Christianity and home of the seat of the Roman Catholic Church from the first Holy Year (1300), it has maintained its cosmopolitan appeal. Geographically and psychologically, the city is closer to the laid-back south than to the can-do north of Italy. Yet Rome is not a city that stands still. In the 27 centuries of its existence, it has seen empires rise and fall, popes and caesars come and go and artistic movements flourish

⊘ THE SEVEN HILLS

Rome is built on seven hills – Aventine, Capitoline, Caelian, Esquiline, Palatine, Quirinal and Viminale – around the River Tiber, 35km (22 miles) from the sea. The city, the *Comune di Roma,* has a population of about 2.7 million and occupies 1,507 sq km (582 sq miles) including the independent city-state of the Vatican, which takes up less than 0.5 sq km (0.19 sq miles). On the same latitude as New York, Rome has a mild climate, but summers can be hot, so the best time to visit is in spring or early autumn.

and fade. As a modern European capital, it cannot rest on its laurels. Rome must play the part of an up-to-date political and business city, while attempting to preserve its unparalleled cultural heritage.

PUBLIC WORKS

Visitors may be bowled over by these treasures, but today's Romans take them in their stride. They are accustomed to conducting their lives against this awe-

The city is packed with tourists in the summer

some backdrop, drinking tap water from an aqueduct constructed by a Roman consul and restored by a Renaissance pope. Perhaps Romans take Rome too much for granted. While it is refreshing that the city is not treated as an open-air museum, sometimes the locals' apparent indifference to the beauty that surrounds them can be grating. Medieval Romans burned marble statues to obtain lime; modern Romans' love affair with the car does almost as much damage. Fumes and traffic vibration have had a terrible impact on the city's monuments. But the damage doesn't all come from the surface. In 2013, geologists started mapping the labyrinth of subterranean tunnels (old tufa quarries) far below the city, which date back to the founding of Rome. In 2013 alone, over 80 structures on the surface collapsed due to this underground network of passages.

Rome's mayors have all tried to improve tourism-related services. Around the year 2000, the Jubilee year, a programme

Characterful Trastevere

of public works was devised to enhance the city's status and restore monuments, archaeological sites and churches. Museums were revamped, and their hours extended. Church facades were given face-lifts. The economic crisis slowed things down, and between 2008 and 2013 Rome's cultural life suffered from severe budget cuts under right-wing mayor Gianni Alemanno. His successor, Ignazio Marino, promised to support culture, tourism, and environmental policy. In August 2013, he banned traffic from the Colosseum portion of Via die Fori Imperiali. Meanwhile, the anti-establishment Virginia Raggi was elected mayor in 2016 and pledged to be 'a mayor for all Romans' and to 'restore legality and transparency to the city's institutions after 20 years of poor governance'.

DAILY LIFE

Visitors should not worry about following the maxim of 'when in Rome...' The rhythms of the Roman day will oblige you to do as the Romans do. For instance, you'll soon discover that there is no point in trying to toil round the sights in the summer afternoon heat. This is the time to join the locals seeking the shade of Rome's parks, or else soak up the atmosphere in a piazza and enjoy one of the refreshing drinks the Romans do so well. A cool *grattachecca* made from grated ice and syrup, or a creamy frullato fruit shake, will do nicely.

⊘ PRINCIPAL ARTISTS AND ARCHITECTS

Bernini, Gian Lorenzo (1598–1680). The foremost exponent of Baroque. Works include St Peter's Square, Fountain of the Four Rivers in Piazza Navona, Palazzo Barberini and Galleria Borghese.

Borromini, Francesco (1599–1667). Baroque architect. He designed Sant'Agnese in Agone, Sant'Ivo alla Sapienza and the Palazzo Barberini.

Bramante, Donato (1444–1514). The foremost architect of the High Renaissance created the Belvedere Courtyard in the Vatican Museums.

Caravaggio, Michelangelo Merisi da (1571–1610). Known for his bold use of foreshortening, dramatic chiaroscuro and earthy realism. His paintings are in Santa Maria del Popolo, San Luigi dei Francesi, Palazzo Barberini, Sant'Agostino, and Galleria Borghese.

Michelangelo Buonarroti (1475–1564). Sculptor, architect, painter. His creations include the dome of St Peter's Basilica, the Sistine Chapel ceiling, *Moses* in the Church of St Peter in Chains, and the Campidoglio.

Pinturicchio, Bernardino (c.1454–1513). Painter of frescoes in the Sistine Chapel, the Borgia Apartments and Santa Maria del Popolo.

Raphael (Raffaello Sanzio) (1483–1520). Painter and architect of the High Renaissance. Works include the *Stanze di Raffaello* in the Vatican, Chigi Chapel in Santa Maria del Popolo, and *La Fornarina* in Palazzo Barberini.

A BRIEF HISTORY

Legend claims that Rome was founded by Romulus, who was sired with his twin brother Remus by the god Mars of a vestal virgin and left on the Palatine Hill to be suckled by a she-wolf. Historians date the founding of the city at 753 BC.

Archaeologists have further established that the site was occupied from the Bronze Age, around 1500 BC. By the 8th century BC villages had sprung up on the Palatine and Aventine hills, and soon after on the Esquiline and Quirinal ridges. These spots proved favourable since they were easily defensible and lay close to where the River Tiber could be forded. After conquering their neighbours, the Romans merged the villages into a single city and surrounded it with a defensive wall. The marshland below the Capitoline Hill was drained and became the Forum.

THE REPUBLIC

A revolt by Roman nobles in 510 BC overthrew the last Etruscan king and established the Republic that was to last for the next five centuries. At first the Republic, under the leadership of two patrician consuls, was plagued by confrontations between patrician (aristocratic) and plebeian (popular) factions. Eventually the plebeians put forward their own leaders, the tribunes, and a solid political order evolved.

In 390 BC, the Gauls besieged the city, destroying everything but the citadel on the Capitoline Hill. When the Gauls left, the hardy citizens set about reconstructing, this time enclosing their city behind a wall of huge tufa blocks. For more than eight centuries, no foreign invader breached those walls.

Rome now extended its control to all of Italy, consolidating its hold with six military roads fanning out from the city – Appia,

Romulus and Remus suckled by a she-wolf

Latina, Salaria, Flaminia, Aurelia and Cassia. By 250 BC, the city's population had grown to 100,000. Victory over Carthage in the Punic Wars (264–146 BC) and conquests in Macedonia, Asia Minor, Spain and southern France, extended Roman power in the Mediterranean. When Hannibal crossed the Alps and invaded Italy in the Second Punic War, large areas of the peninsula were devastated and peasants sought refuge in Rome, swelling the population still further.

The acquisition of largely unsought territories brought new social and economic problems. Unemployment, poor housing and an inadequate public works programme provoked unrest within the city. Civil wars shook the Republic, which ultimately yielded to dictatorship. Julius Caesar, a former proconsul who had achieved some fame by subduing Gaul and Britain, crossed the tiny Rubicon River, which marked the boundary of his province, and marched boldly on Rome to seize power.

THE EMPIRE

Caesar sought to combat unemployment and ease the tax burden, but his reforms bypassed the Senate and he made dangerous enemies. His assassination on the Ides of March in 44 BC led to civil war and to the despotic rule of his adopted son Octavian, who, as Augustus, became the first emperor (see page 53). Under Augustus, *Pax Romana* – the peace, or rather the rule of Rome – held together the far-flung Empire. To make Rome a worthy capital, he added fine public buildings in the form of baths, theatres and temples, claiming he had "found Rome brick and left it marble". He also introduced public services, including the first fire brigade. This was the Golden Age of Roman letters, distinguished by poets and historians; Horace, Livy, Ovid and Virgil.

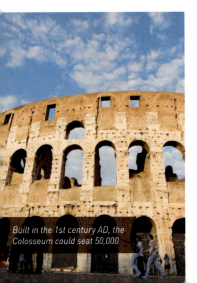

Built in the 1st century AD, the Colosseum could seat 50,000

In the first centuries of the Empire, tens of thousands of foreigners flooded into Rome, among them the first Christians, including St Peter and St Paul. The emperors tried to suppress this 'new religion', but the steadfastness of its adherents and their willingness to become martyrs increased its appeal.

Each of Augustus' successors contributed his own embellishments to Rome. In the rebuilding after a disastrous fire ravaged the city in AD 64,

Nero provided himself with an ostentatious villa, the Domus Aurea (Golden House), on the Esquiline Hill. Hadrian reconstructed the Pantheon, raised a monumental mausoleum for himself (Castel Sant'Angelo), and retired to his magnificent estate, Villa Adriana at Tivoli.

In the late 1st and 2nd centuries AD Rome reached its peak, with a population of over one million. Inherent flaws in the imperial system, however, began to weaken the emperor's power and eventually led to the downfall of the Empire.

After the death of Septimius Severus in AD 211, 25 emperors reigned in just 74 years, many of them assassinated. Fire and plague took their toll on the city's population. In 283 the Forum was almost completely destroyed by fire and never recovered its former magnificence.

After a vision of the Cross appeared to him on a battlefield, the story goes, Emperor Constantine I converted to Christianity. He ensured that Christianity was tolerated by an edict passed in 313, and he built the first churches and basilicas in Rome. In 331 he effectively split the Empire in two when he moved the imperial seat to Byzantium (Constantinople, modern Istanbul). Many of the wealthy, as well as talented artists, joined him and the old capital never recovered.

THE FALL OF ROME

As the Western Empire went into decline, the Romans recruited northern tribes into the legions to help defend it against other outsiders. But the hired defenders soon deserted, and the disenchanted and weary Roman populace failed to summon up the same enthusiasm to defend the city that they had shown in conquering an empire.

Wave after wave of 'Barbarians' (foreigners) came to sack, rape, murder and pillage; Alaric the Visigoth in 410, Attila the

Hun, the Vandals and the Ostrogoths. Finally the Germanic chief Odoacer forced the last Roman emperor, Romulus Augustulus, to abdicate in 476. The Western Empire was at an end, although the Eastern Empire continued until 1453.

PAPAL POWER

In the 6th century, Justinian re-annexed Italy to the Byzantine Empire and codified Roman law as the state's legal system. But, as later Byzantine emperors lost interest in Rome, a new power arose out of the chaos; the papacy. Pope Leo I (440–61) asserted the Bishop of Rome as Primate of the Western Church, tracing the succession back to St Peter who had been martyred in the city. Pope Gregory the Great (590–604) showed statesmanship in warding off the Lombards, a Germanic tribe already established in the north of Italy. In the 8th century, citing a document, the *Donation of Constantine* (later found to be a forgery), the popes began to claim authority over all of Italy.

Seeking the support of the powerful Franks, Pope Leo III crowned their king, Charlemagne, emperor in St Peter's Basilica on Christmas Day 800. But the Pope in turn had to kneel in allegiance to the Emperor, and this exchange of spiritual blessing for military protection sowed the seeds

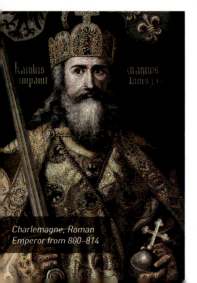

Charlemagne, Roman Emperor from 800–814

of future conflict between the papacy and secular rulers. Over the next 400 years, Italy saw invasions by Saracens and Magyars, Saxons and Normans (who sacked Rome in 1084), with papal Rome struggling along as only one of many

Rome abandoned

By the 8th century, Rome had been reduced to just a village. Its small population deserted the city entirely when Barbarian invaders cut the imperial aqueducts.

feudal city-states on the now tormented peninsula. The papacy, and with it Rome, was controlled by various powerful families from the landed nobility. As the situation in Rome degenerated into chaos – deplored by Dante in his *Divine Comedy* – the popes fled in 1309 to comfortable exile in Avignon, and remained under the protection of the French king until 1377. Rome was left to the brutal rule of the Orsini and Colonna families.

THE RENAISSANCE

Returning to Rome, the popes harshly put down any resistance to their rule and remained dominant in the city for the next 400 years. During the 15th and 16th centuries, the papacy became a notable patron of the Renaissance, that remarkable effusion of art and intellectual endeavour which transformed medieval Rome from a squalid, crumbling and fever-ridden backwater to one of the foremost cities of the Christian world.

It was Giorgio Vasari, facile artist and first-rate chronicler of this cultural explosion, who dubbed this movement a *rinascita*, or rebirth of the glories of Italy's Greco-Roman past. The father of Rome's High Renaissance, Pope Julius II (1503–13), was responsible for the new St Peter's Basilica. He also commissioned Michelangelo to paint the ceiling of the Sistine Chapel and Raphael to decorate the Vatican's Stanze. Donato

Bramante, the architect, got the nickname *maestro ruinante* because of the countless ancient monuments he had dismantled for the Pope's megalomaniacal building plans. With the treasures uncovered during this process, Julius founded the Vatican's magnificent collection of ancient sculpture.

But the exuberant life of Renaissance Rome was extinguished in May 1527 by the arrival of the German troops of Holy Roman Emperor Charles V; the last – and worst – sacking of the city.

In the mid-17th century, Martin Luther, John Calvin and other leaders of the Reformation challenged the papacy and the doctrines of the Church of Rome. A Counter-Reformation was proclaimed in 1563, reinforcing the Holy Office's Inquisition to combat heresy and the Index to censor the arts. Protestants fled and Jews were shut up in a ghetto. Art proved a major instrument of Counter-Reformation propaganda. As the Church regained ground, it replaced the pagan influences of classicism with a more triumphant image, epitomised by Bernini's grand Baroque altar canopy in St Peter's. The Baroque flourished in Rome as in no other Italian city.

Garibaldi monument in Piazza Garibaldi

THE HABSBURGS

In the 18th century, Spain's authority over many of

Italy's states passed to the Habsburgs of Austria, who were determined to curb papal power in Rome. The influential order of Jesuits was dissolved, while Habsburg church reforms meant a crippling loss of revenue and the papacy lost prestige.

In 1798 Napoleon's troops entered Rome, later seized the Papal States and proclaimed a Republic. They treated Pius VI with contempt and carried him off to be a virtual prisoner in France. His successor, Pius VII, was forced to proclaim Napoleon as emperor and was also made prisoner.

During the French occupation, a national self-awareness began to develop among Italians to challenge foreign rule. Many looked to Pope Pius IX to lead a nationalist movement, but he feared the spread of liberalism and when Giuseppe Mazzini set up a Republic in Rome in 1848, the Pope fled. He returned the following year, after the fall of the Republic.

National unity was achieved in 1860 through the shrewd diplomacy of Prime Minister Cavour, the heroics of a guerrilla general, Giuseppe Garibaldi, and the leadership of King Vittorio Emanuele of Piedmont. Rome became capital of Italy in 1871 and Pope Pius IX retreated to the Vatican, a 'prisoner of the monarchy'.

THE MODERN ERA

In World War I Italy sided with the allies against Austria and Germany. But after the peace conference of 1919, disarray on the political scene led to an economic crisis, with stagnant productivity, bank closures and rising unemployment. From this turmoil the Fascist movement grew, and when the *fascisti* marched on Rome in 1922, King Vittorio Emanuele III invited their leader, Benito Mussolini (*Il Duce*), to form a government. Once in power, Mussolini made peace with the Pope through the Lateran Treaty of 1929, which created a separate Vatican State and perpetuated Roman Catholicism as the national religion. In 1940 Mussolini sided with Hitler in World War II, but the Allies declared Rome an open city to spare it from bombing. It was liberated in 1944, intact.

POST-WAR 'MIRACLE'

The initial post-war period was a time of hardship, but the 1950s saw Rome enjoying Italy's 'economic miracle'. Celebrities made the city their playground, finding *la dolce vita* in the nightspots of the Via Veneto. Rome's population soared, as immigrants from the south came in search of work.

In the 1970s, the city weathered a storm of both left- and right-wing political terrorism, and the decade became known as Italy's *anni di piombo* ('years of lead'). The darkest hour came in 1978 when the Red Brigades kidnapped and murdered the former Prime Minister, Aldo Moro.

Changes are being made to make city services more efficient, and authorities are attempting to tackle pollution and traffic congestion. In August 2013, newly elected centre-left mayor Ignazio Marino turned via dei Fori Imperiali into a huge pedestrian area, allowing only bus and taxi circulation. In late 2014 the Rome corruption scandal was uncovered when an organised crime network attempted to approach Mayor Ignazio Marino who reported them to the authorities. Among those investigated for embezzling public funds are the former mayor of Rome Gianni Alemanno and many prominent Italian politicians and businessmen. In 2015, Italy's Senate passed an anti-corruption bill heightening the penalties for accounting fraud, civil service corruption and mafia crime. A year later, riding a wave of discontent aimed at the political elite, Virginia Raggi of the populist Five Star Movement (M5S) became the first woman in history to be elected Mayor of Rome, and opened a new chapter in the city's history.

HISTORICAL LANDMARKS

753 BC Foundation of Rome.

510 BC Expulsion of Etruscans. Roman Republic established.

31 BC Augustus becomes first Roman emperor.

AD 69–79 Emperor Vespasian has the Colosseum built.

98–117 The Empire achieves its greatest expansion under Trajan.

395 The Empire is divided between West and East.

476 Fall of the Western Roman Empire..

1309–77 The papacy moves to Avignon, France.

15th century Rome prospers during the Renaissance, attracting such masters as Botticelli, Caravaggio, Michelangelo, Raphael and Titian.

1527 Army of Charles V of Spain sacks Rome.

1585–90 Pope Sixtus V commissions Fontana, Bernini, Borromini and Maderno to build churches, palaces, squares and fountains.

17th century The Italian peninsula fragments into numerous smaller states, among them the Papal States, with Rome as their capital.

1801 Under Napoleon, Rome is made part of the French Empire.

1915 Italy joins Allies in World War I.

1922 Mussolini's march on Rome.

1940 Italy joins Germany in World War II.

1944 Rome liberated. King Vittorio Emanuele III abdicates.

1957 Fledgling European Union established under Treaty of Rome.

2005 Pope John Paul II dies. Pope Benedict XVI elected.

2008 Silvio Berlusconi elected prime minister for the third time.

2011 Pope John Paul II beatified. Berlusconi resigns over debt crisis.

2013 Benedict XVI retires and is succeeded by Pope Francis

2014 Pope John Paul II is canonised. Democrat Matteo Renzi forms new government.

2015 Italy's Senate backs a new, more stringent anti-corruption bill.

2016 Two powerful earthquakes hit central Italy killing hundreds and displacing tens of thousands. Virginia Raggi is elected Rome's first female mayor. Renzi calls a referendum on constitutional reform, but is defeated and resigns shortly after.

Rome's main gathering point: the Spanish Steps

WHERE TO GO

Visitors to Rome soon discover that cultural residues from different eras are often interwoven: a pagan mausoleum is also a papal fortress, a medieval church has a Baroque facade, and a Renaissance palace overlooks a modern traffic junction. It doesn't matter whether you've come to Rome for the grandeur of the ancient remains, the revered pilgrimage sites of the Catholic Church or the inspired works of Michelangelo, Raphael and Bernini – you'll end up seeing a glorious hotchpotch of them all.

Although the municipality of Rome sprawls over a huge area, the principal sights are packed into a comparatively small zone. For the most part, the best way of getting about is on foot. Much of the historic centre has been closed to traffic and parking is generally impossible. Rome's public transport has been improved and although crowded during rush hours, it will usually get you near enough to your destination.

PIAZZA VENEZIA AND CAPITOLINE HILL

The most convenient place to begin exploring is **Piazza Venezia ❶**. The hub of the capital's main traffic arteries, this is a principal stop on several major bus routes and close to a number of sites. As far as orientation is concerned, the **Vittoriano** (Vittorio Emanuele Monument; www.polo

Closed Mondays

Many museums are closed on Mondays (the Forum, Colosseum, Palatine and the Vatican museums are notable exceptions), 1 January and 25 December. In the majority of cases, last entry is one hour before closing.

The gleaming white Vittoriano Monument

musealelazio.beniculturali.it; daily 9.30am–5.30pm, until 4.30pm in winter; free) is a landmark visible from all over the city, and provides one of the best views of central Rome. Romans wish the dazzling white marble monument were not quite so conspicuous, however, and heap upon it such derisive nicknames as 'Rome's False Teeth' and 'The Wedding Cake'. Built from 1885 to 1911 to celebrate the unification of Italy and dedicated to the new nation's first king, the Vittoriano contains the **Altare della Patria**, the tomb of Italy's Unknown Soldier of World War I. The monument also has a museum complex, with important temporary art exhibitions in its western wing (www.ilvittoriano.com). Once you have climbed to the Altare della Patria, a lift offers access to a panorama of the city (daily 9.30am–6.45pm).

A much more impressive work of architecture on the west side of the piazza **Palazzo Venezia**, is the first great

Renaissance palace in Rome (www.museopalazzovenezia. beniculturali.it; Tue–Sun 8.30am–7.30pm, ticket office until 6.30pm). It was once the embassy of the Venetian Republic to the Holy See, and in the 20th century served as Mussolini's headquarters. His desk stood at the far corner of the Sala del Mappamondo, positioned to intimidate visitors, who had to approach across 21 metres (70ft) of marble floor. From the balcony over the central door, *Il Duce* harangued crowds in the square below. The palace contains a museum of medieval and Renaissance furniture, arms, tapestries, ceramics and sculpture.

◉ THE FIRST CAPITOL HILL

To the Romans, the Capitol was both citadel and sanctuary, the symbolic centre of government, where the consuls took their oath and the Republic's coinage was minted. Its name originated when a human skull was unearthed during excavations for the Temple of Jupiter and interpreted as a sign that Rome would one day be head *(caput)* of the world.

When the Gauls sacked Rome in 390 BC, the Capitol was saved by the timely cackling of the sanctuary's sacred geese, warning that attackers were scaling the rocks. Later, victorious caesars ended their triumphal processions here. They rode up from the Forum in chariots drawn by white horses to pay homage at the magnificent gilded Temple of Jupiter, which dominated the southern tip of the Capitoline.

In the Middle Ages, the collapsed temples were pillaged and the hill was abandoned to goats until, in the 16th century, Pope Paul III commissioned Michelangelo to give the Campidoglio its new glory.

CAPITOLINE HILL

Two flights of steps lead up behind the Vittorio Emanuele Monument. The more graceful, **La Cordonata**, takes you up between statues of Castor and Pollux (mythical twin sons of Leda and the Swan) to the tranquil elegance of the **Piazza del Campidoglio** on top of the **Capitoline Hill**.

This was once the Capitol, where the Temple of Jupiter Optimus Maximus Capitolinus stood, ancient Rome's most sacred site. Today the Campidoglio is a fine Renaissance square, designed by Michelangelo (who also designed La Cordonata) for the reception of the Holy Roman Emperor Charles V. Michelangelo also remodelled the existing **Palazzo Senatorio**, Rome's former town hall, and planned the two palaces that flank it, the Palazzo dei Conservatori and the Palazzo Nuovo, which were completed after his death. Michelangelo had the magnificent 2nd century AD bronze **statue of Marcus Aurelius** placed in the square. The statue is a copy: the original is the centrepiece of the glass-covered **Sala Marco Aurelio** in the Musei Capitolini. The statue survived destruction after the decline of Rome because it was mistaken for a likeness of the Christian emperor Constantine, rather than of the pagan Marcus Aurelius.

The **Musei Capitolini** ❷ (www.museicapitolini.org; daily 9.30am–7.30pm, last entry 6.30pm) in the palaces of the Campidoglio, have extensive collections of sculpture excavated from ancient Rome. Enter through the courtyard of the **Palazzo dei Conservatori**, where you will encounter a giant marble head, hand and foot, fragments from a 12-metre (40ft) statue of Emperor Constantine II. The palace is also home to the *Capitoline She-Wolf* depicted suckling the infants Romulus and Remus. This Etruscan bronze has become the symbol of Rome. In the top-floor **Pinacoteca Capitolina** (Capitoline Picture Gallery) are fine works by Caravaggio, Tintoretto, Velázquez, Rubens and Titian.

An underground passageway lined with artefacts connects the Palazzo dei Conservatori with the **Palazzo Nuovo**. The latter contains rows of portrait busts of Roman emperors, although its highlights are the poignant statue of the *Dying Gaul*, the sensual *Capitoline Venus*, a Roman copy of a Greek original dating from the 2nd century BC, and the *Marble Faun*.

Bronze statue of Constantine, Palazzo dei Conservatori

Alongside the Palazzo Senatorio a cobbled road opens out onto a terrace, giving you the best view of the Roman Forum ruins (see page 31), stretching from the Arch of Septimius Severus to the Arch of Titus, with the Colosseum beyond. The steeper flight of steps up the Campidoglio climbs to the church of **Santa Maria in Aracoeli** on the site of the temple of Juno Moneta. The 13th-century church is the home of the much-revered *Santo Bambino* (Baby Jesus), kept in a separate chapel. The original statue, believed to have miraculous powers, was stolen in 1994 and has been replaced with a copy.

ANCIENT ROME

The heart of ancient Rome is around the Colosseum (see page 38), with the Imperial Fora and Roman Forum to the northwest and the Baths of Caracalla (see page 39) to the south. Don't try to decipher each fragment of broken stone – not even archaeologists have succeeded. It's far better to soak up the romantic atmosphere while reflecting on the ruined majesty of this ancient civilisation. Take care to avoid summer's midday sun, as the Forum provides no shade.

THE IMPERIAL FORA

Begin at the **Fori Imperiali** (Imperial Fora), which were built as an adjunct to the Foro Romano in honour of Julius Caesar, Augustus, Trajan, Vespasian and Nerva. At the northern end of Trajan's Forum stands the remarkable 30-metre (100ft) **Trajan's Column** (Colonna Traiana; AD 113). Celebrating Trajan's campaigns against the Dacians in what is now Romania, the intricate friezes spiralling round the column constitute a veritable textbook of Roman warfare, featuring embarkation on ships, the clash of armies and the surrender of Barbarian chieftains – in all, using some 2,500 figures. St Peter's statue atop the column replaced the Emperor's in 1587.

At **Trajan's Forum** (Foro di Traiano), which can only be viewed from Via dei Fori Imperiali, you can see some of the best preserved ancient Roman streets and the semi-circular **Trajan's Markets** ❸ (Mercati di Traiano), an ancient shopping mall, made up of 150 shops and offices. The multi-tiered **Trajan's Forum Museum** (www.mercatiditraiano.it; daily 9.30am–7.30pm, last entry 6.30pm) provides an insight into the history and restoration of the site. A **Tourist Information Point**

Combination ticket

The combination ticket that covers entry into the Colosseum, Palatine Hill and the Roman Forum is valid two days. Buying it online at www.coopculture.it should save queuing time. Another possibility is the seven-day Archeologia Card, which covers even more ancient sites.

Trajan's Markets

(www.turismoroma.it; daily 9.30am–7pm; free) on the Via dei Fori Imperiali, between Via Cavour and the Colosseum metro stop, gives useful information about the Imperial Fora and ongoing excavation work there.

THE ROMAN FORUM

You can stand among the columns, porticoes and arches of the **Roman Forum ❹** (Foro Romano; www.coopculture.it; 8.30am–1 hour before sunset, until 7.15pm in full summer and 4.30pm in winter) and, with an exhilarating leap of the imagination, picture the hub of the great Imperial City. Surrounded by the Palatine, Capitoline and Esquiline hills, the flat valley of the Forum developed as the civic, commercial and religious centre of the city. Under the emperors, it attained unprecedented splendour, with white marble and golden roofs of temples, law courts and market halls glittering in the sun.

After the Barbarian invasions, the area was abandoned. Subsequent fire, earthquakes, floods and plunder by Renaissance architects reduced the area to a muddy cow pasture, until excavations in the 19th century once again brought many of the ancient edifices to light. Grass still grows between the cracked paving stones of the Via Sacra, poppies bloom among the piles of toppled marble and tangles of red roses are entwined in the brick columns, softening the harshness of the ruins.

Audio-guides can be hired at the entrance on Via dei Fori Imperiali at Piazza Santa Maria Nova 53, or you can find your own way around. Before you begin, make yourself comfortable on a chunk of fallen marble among the ruins and orientate yourself with a detailed map, so that you can trace the layout of the ruins and make sense of the apparent confusion.

Ideally, start at the west end, just below the Campidoglio's Palazzo Senatorio (see page 28). Here you can see how the arches of the Roman record office (*Tabularium*) have been incorporated into the rear of the Renaissance palace. Look along the length of the **Via Sacra** (Sacred Way), the route taken by generals as they rode in triumphal procession to the foot of the Capitoline Hill, followed by the legions' standards, ranks of prisoners and carts piled with the spoils of war.

The First Senate House

To counterbalance this image of the Romans as ruthless military conquerors, turn to the brick-built **Curia**, home of the Roman Senate, in the Forum's northwest corner. Here you can gaze through the bronze doors (copies of the originals, which are now in the church of San Giovanni in Laterano; see page 78) at the 'venerable great-grandmother of all parliaments', where the senators, robed in togas, argued the affairs of Republic and Empire. The tenets of Roman law, which

The Temple of Saturn

underpin most European legal systems, were first debated here. Diocletian constructed the present building in AD 303. Its plain brick facade was once faced with marble. The church that covered it was dismantled in 1937 to reveal an ancient floor set with geometrical patterns in red and green marble, as well as tiers on either side where the senators sat, and the brick base of the golden statue of Victory at the rear. The Curia shelters two bas-reliefs, outlining in marble the buildings of the Forum.

In front of the Curia, a concrete shelter protects the underground site of the **Lapis Niger** (usually not on view), a black marble stone placed by Silla over the (presumed) grave of Romulus, the city's founder. Beside it is a stele engraved with the oldest Latin inscription ever found, dating back to the 6th century BC; it has not yet been deciphered.

The triple **Arco di Settimio Severo** (Arch of Septimius Severus) dominates this end of the Forum. Its friezes depict the eastern military triumphs of the 3rd-century emperor who later campaigned as far as Scotland. Nearby is the orators' platform, or **Rostra**. Its name comes from the iron prows (*rostra*) that once adorned it, taken from enemy ships at the Battle of Antium in 338 BC. Two points in the Rostra have particular significance: the *Umbilicus Urbis Romae* marks the traditional epicentre of Rome, and the *Miliarium Aureum* (Golden Milestone) recorded in gold letters the distances in miles from Rome to the cities of the far-flung Empire.

Public meetings and ceremonies took place in front of the Rostra, kept bare save for samples of three plants considered sacred to Mediterranean prosperity: the vine, the olive and the fig. Still prominent above this open space is the **Colonna di Foca** (Column of Phocas), built to honour the Byzantine emperor who presented the Pantheon to Pope Boniface IV.

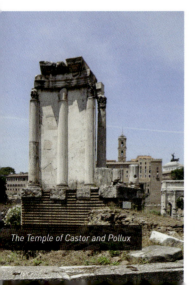

The Temple of Castor and Pollux

Eight tall columns standing on a podium at the foot of the Capitol belong to the **Tempio di Saturno** (Temple of Saturn), one of the earliest temples in Rome. It doubled as both state treasury and centre of the December debauchery known as the Saturnalia, the pagan precursor of Christmas.

Of the **Basilica Giulia**, which was once busy law courts named after Julius Caesar who commissioned it, only the paving and some of the arches and travertine pillars survive. Even less remains of the Basilica Aemilia, on the opposite side of the Via Sacra, destroyed by the Goths in AD 410.

Three columns, the podium and part of the entablature denote the **Tempio dei Castori** (Temple of Castor and Pollux), built in 484 BC. It was dedicated to the twin sons of Leda and the Swan, after they appeared at Lake Regillus to rally the Romans against the Latins and Etruscans.

Caesar's End

The altar of Julius Caesar is tucked away in a semicircular recess of the **Tempio di Giulio Cesare** (Temple of Julius Caesar). On 19 March in 44 BC, the grieving crowds, following Caesar's funeral procession to his cremation in the Campus Martius, made an impromptu pyre of chairs and tables and burned his body in the Forum instead.

Pause for a pleasant idyll in the **Casa delle Vestali** (House of the Vestal Virgins), surrounded by graceful statues in the serene setting of a rose garden and old rectangular fountain basins, once more filled with water. In the circular white marble **Tempio di Vesta** (Temple of Vesta), the sacred flame perpetuating the Roman state was tended by six Vestal Virgins who, from childhood, observed a 30-year vow of chastity under threat of being buried alive if they broke it. They were supervised by the high priest, the Pontifex Maximus (the popes have since appropriated this title), of which only brick vestiges remain.

The imposing **Tempio di Antonino e Faustina** (Temple of Antoninus and Faustina), further along the Via Sacra, has survived because, like the Curia, it was converted into a church, acquiring a Baroque facade in 1602. Few ancient buildings can match the massive proportions of the **Basilica di Massenzio**

(Basilica of Maxentius), started by Maxentius and completed by Constantine. Three giant vaults still stand.

The Via Sacra culminates in the **Arco di Tito** (Arch of Titus), built to commemorate the capture of Jerusalem in AD 70. Restored by Giuseppe Valadier in 1821, it shows in magnificent carved relief the triumphal procession of Titus bearing the spoils of the city, among them the Temple of Jerusalem's altar, a seven-branched golden menorah and silver trumpets.

THE PALATINE HILL

From this end of the Forum a slope leads up to the **Palatine Hill ⑤** (Palatino; www.coopculture.it; daily 8.30am–1 hour before sunset, until 7.15pm in full summer and 4.30pm in winter). Rome's legendary birthplace and today its most romantic garden, is dotted with toppled columns among the wild flowers and spiny acanthus shrubs. At the time of the ancient Republic, this was a desirable residential district for the wealthy and aristocratic, including Cicero and Crassus. Augustus began the Imperial trend and later emperors added and expanded, each trying to outdo the last until the whole area was one immense palace (hence the name of the hill). From the pavilions and terraces of the 16th-century gardens laid out here by the Farnese family, there is a superb view of the whole Forum. A small **museum** (follow the signs) displays artefacts found nearby.

Just west of the gardens is the **Casa di Augusto** (House of Augustus), where Augustus lived in around 30 BC before he gained supreme power and built his imperial palace complex just along the hill. The rooms with their exquisite frescoes in red, blue and ochre, were opened after years of painstaking restoration. The **Casa di Livia** (House of Livia), which was occupied by his ambitious and scheming wife, also has some fine frescoes and wall mosaics. Both houses can be visited only on by guided tours (booking required, see www.coopculture. it). Nearby, three circular Iron-Age dwellings unearthed from the time of Rome's legendary beginnings are known as the **Capanne di Romolo** (Romulus' Huts).

A passageway, the **Criptoportico**, linked the Palatine buildings to Nero's palace, the **Domus Aurea**. In the dim light you can just make out stucco decorations on the ceilings and walls at one end.

The vast assemblage of ruins of the **Domus Flavia** includes a basilica, throne room, banqueting hall, baths, porticoes and a fountain in the form of a maze. Together with the **Domus Augustana**, the complex is known as the **Palace of Domitian**. You can look down into the Stadium of Domitian, which was probably a venue for horse races.

The last emperor to build on the Palatine, Septimius Severus, carried the imperial palace right to the hill's south-eastern end, so that his **Domus Severiana** was the impressive first glimpse of the capital for new arrivals. It was dismantled and its expanses of marble were used to build Renaissance Rome.

From this edge of the hill you have a great view down into the immense grassy stretch of the **Circus Maximus ❻**, where vast crowds watched chariot races from tiers of marble seats.

Inside the Colosseum

THE COLOSSEUM

It says something about the earthiness of Rome that, more than any church or palace, it is the **Colosseum** ❼ that is the symbol of the city's eternity (Colosseo; http://archeoroma. beniculturali.it; daily 8.30am–1 hour before sunset, until 7.15pm in full summer and 4.30pm in winter). Built in AD 72–80, the four-tiered elliptical amphitheatre seated some 50,000 spectators on stone benches, according to social status.

The gladiators were originally criminals, war captives and slaves: later, free men entered the 'profession', tempted by wealth and fame. Contrary to popular belief, there is little historical evidence to support the image of the Colosseum as the place where Christians were fed to the lions. The first stage of the restoration was completed in 2016, which saw the reopening of the underground, hypogeum and the third ring, boasting incredible views of the city (www.coopculture.it; 9am–5pm, shorter hours in winter; guided tours only).

Popes and princes stripped the Colosseum of its marble cladding, and its travertine and metal for their churches and palaces. They have left behind a ruined maze of cells and corridors that funnelled men and beasts to the slaughter. The horror has disappeared beneath the moss, but the thrill of the monument's endurance remains. As an Anglo-Saxon prophecy says: "While stands the Colosseum, Rome shall stand; when falls the Colosseum, Rome shall fall; and when Rome falls, with it shall fall the world."

The nearby **Arco di Costantino** (Arch of Constantine) celebrates Constantine's victory over his imperial rival Maxentius at Saxa Rubra. He may have won the battle, but a cost-conscious Senate decorate the arch with pieces from monuments of earlier rulers Trajan, Hadrian and Marcus Aurelius.

Immediately northeast of the Colosseum is the **Domus Aurea** (www.coop culture.it; only Sat–Sun 9am–5pm, guided tours only, booking required), once a glorious 250-room villa with extensive gardens built by the emperor Nero, who spent very few years in his 'Golden House' before killing himself in AD 68. Very little is left of the lavish mosaics, frescoes, inlaid floors and paintings in gold.

The Arch of Constantine

BATHS OF CARACALLA

The huge 3rd-century AD **Terme di Caracalla** ❽, 1km (0.6 miles) south of the Colosseum, were built for people to bathe in considerable style and luxury (http://archeoroma.beni culturali.it or www.coopculture.it; Mon 9am–2pm, Tue–Sun 9am–1 hour before sunset; ticket office closes 1 hour earlier). Public bathing was a prolonged social event. Senators and merchants passed from the *caldarium* (hot room) to cool down in the *tepidarium* and the *frigidarium*. The baths ran dry in the 6th century when Barbarians cut the aqueducts. Now, in the summer, the baths become the setting for spectacular open-air operas. In the past, the ruins themselves were used for lighting and stage purposes, but in today's more preservation-conscious times, a separate structure is built in the grounds and the ruins serve as a majestic backdrop.

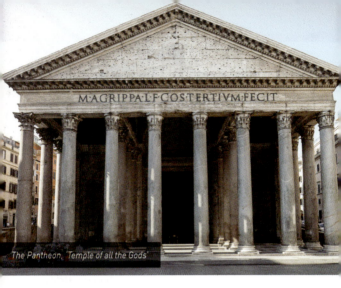
The Pantheon, Temple of all the Gods

CENTRO STORICO

The heart of Rome's historic centre is the area enclosed by the bend of the River Tiber. Here, on what was once the exercise ground of Roman soldiers known as the Campus Martius or 'Field of Mars', you will find vestiges of Rome's many different eras. Next to the remains of ancient temples there is a maze of medieval streets, as well as graceful Renaissance *palazzi*, ornate Baroque churches, sublime piazzas and spectacular fountains. But the city centre is up-to-date, too – among the monuments are contemporary shops, hotels and the businesses of modern Rome.

THE PANTHEON

The magnificent **Pantheon** ❾ (www.polomusealelazio.benicul turali.it; Mon–Sat 9am–7.30pm, Sun until 6pm; free) in the Piazza della Rotonda is ancient Rome's best-preserved monument. This

'Temple of All the Gods', and its elegant hemispherical dome that has become a city landmark, was saved for posterity when it was converted into a church in the 7th century. The original Pantheon, built in 27 BC by Marcus Agrippa (son-in-law of Augustus), burned down. Emperor Hadrian rebuilt it around AD 125, but modestly left his predecessor's name on the frieze above the portico, supported by 16 monolithic pink-and-grey granite columns. The bronze beams that once adorned the entrance were taken away by the Barberini Pope Urban VIII to make Bernini's *baldacchino* canopy for the high altar in St Peter's. His action prompted the saying: "*Quod non fecerunt barbari, fecerunt Barberini*" ("What the Barbarians didn't do, the Barberini did").

The Pantheon's true greatness is only fully appreciated once you step inside and look up into the magnificent coffered **dome**. Over 43 metres (141ft) in diameter (exactly equal to its height), it is even wider than the cupola of St Peter's Basilica. Held up without any sustaining columns or flying–buttresses, it is an unparalleled feat of engineering. On fine days a shaft of sunlight illuminates the windowless vault through the circular hole *(oculus)* in the dome. The gods and goddesses are long gone, replaced by the Renaissance tombs of Raphael (and his mistress) and the architect Baldassarre Peruzzi, as well as the first king of Italy.

PIAZZA NAVONA

A short walk west of the Pantheon is the beautiful **Piazza Navona** ⓾, the heart of the northern half of the Centro Storico and a prime spot for recreation since the time of Emperor Domitian, who laid out an athletics arena, Circus Agonalis, on this site in AD 79, establishing the future piazza's oval shape.

Jousting tournaments took place here in the Middle Ages, and from the 17th to the 19th century it was the scene of spectacular water pageants in summer, when the fountains overflowed until the piazza was flooded. Today the piazza remains Rome's perfect stage set, and the public spectacle continues. Secure a front-row seat at any of the alfresco caffès and enjoy the show supplied by artists, performers, musicians and caricaturists.

The baroque centrepiece of the piazza is Bernini's **Fontana dei Quattro Fiumi** (Fountain of the Four Rivers), which incorporates an ancient obelisk into a monumental allegory symbolising the great rivers of the four continents: the Americas (Río de la Plata), Europe (the Danube), Asia (the Ganges) and Africa (the Nile). Romans who delight in Bernini's scorn for his rivals suggest that the Nile god is covering his head rather than having to look at Borromini's church of Sant'Agnese in Agone, and that the river god of the Americas is poised to catch it in case it collapses. In fact the fountain was completed some years before Borromini's fine facade and dome.

A brief walk north from the piazza will lead to the **Palazzo Altemps ⑪** (Tue–Sun 9am–7.45pm, June–Sept Fri also 8–10pm), a branch of the Museo Nazionale Romano (see page 76), which

⊙ BERNINI AND THE BAROQUE

Although more restrained than elsewhere in Europe, Roman Baroque is theatrical, bold and at times bombastic. At the forefront was architect and sculptor, Gian Lorenzo Bernini (1598–1680), whose style found favour with a succession of popes. Even St Peter's is, in part, a Bernini creation, graced by enfolding, keyhole-shaped colonnades. Other masterpieces include the witty design for an elephant to bear the obelisk of Santa Maria sopra Minerva and the angels on Ponte Sant'Angelo. Palazzo Barberini (1629–33) heralded the Baroque style and was completed by Bernini, assisted by Borromini, who became his arch-rival.

features the magnificent **Boncompagni Ludovisi collection** in a gorgeous 16th-century palace containing frescoed halls, a painted loggia, a church, a theatre and a beautiful internal courtyard. Among the most important pieces is the marble altar top known as the *Ludovisi Throne*, thought to be an original Greek work from the 5th century BC, with exquisitely carved reliefs of Aphrodite and a maiden

Fountain of the Four Rivers in Piazza Navona

playing the flute. Also, seek out the tragic *Suicide of a Galatian*, the statue of a Barbarian warrior in the act of killing himself and his wife rather than submit to slavery. Other highlights include the colossal head of Juno and the equally gigantic sarcophagus featuring intricate scenes of battle between Romans and Barbarians. Victory over the Barbarians was a much-favoured decorative theme between the second half of the 2nd century AD and the first half of the 3rd century AD.

EAST OF THE PANTHEON

In an enchanting setting of russet and ochre rococo housing is the 17th-century church of **Sant'Ignazio** (http://santignazio. gesuiti.it). Inside, Fra Andrea Pozzo (himself a Jesuit priest) painted a *trompe l'oeil* **ceiling fresco** (1685) depicting St Ignatius' entry into paradise. Stand on a buff stone disc in the nave's central aisle and look up; you will have the impression of the building rising above you. From any other point, the columns appear to collapse. From another disc further up the aisle, you can admire the celestial dome above the Baroque altar.

South of here, around the corner from the Piazza del Collegio Romano, is the vast **Palazzo Doria Pamphili** ⑫ (also spelt Pamphilj; Via del Corso 305; www.doriapamphilj.it; daily 9am– 7pm), the private residence of the important Doria family. The family's rich collection of paintings was assembled over hundreds of years. There are a number of masterpieces from the 15th to the 17th century, including works by Raphael, Titian, Tintoretto, Veronese and Caravaggio, as well as paintings from the Dutch and Flemish schools. Look out for the evocative landscape of the *Flight into Egypt* by Annibale Carracci, Caravaggio's *Penitent Magdalen* and the windswept *Naval Battle in the Bay of Naples* by Brueghel the Elder. You'll find a nice stylistic contrast in a little room off to the side of the galleries; Velázquez's brilliant worldly portrait of *Innocent X*, the Pamphili family pope, alongside a more serene marble bust of him by Bernini.

Via dei Pastini

The pedestrian-only Via dei Pastini leads east from the Piazza della Rotonda and forms the beginning of a tourist drag that takes in the columns of the Tempio di Adriano, as well as ice-cream outlets and souvenir shops, before crossing the Via del Corso and eventually reaching the Trevi Fountain (see page 54).

SOUTH OF THE PANTHEON

Streets on either side of the Pantheon lead south to the Largo di Torre Argentina and across the main road to the **Area Sacra Argentina**, the excavated remains of four temples dating from the 3rd to 1st century BC (viewed from the road only).

On the other side of Largo Argentina is **Il Gesù** ⑬,

the mother church of the Jesuits and a major element in their Counter-Reformation campaign. Begun as their Roman headquarters in 1568, its open plan became the model for the congregational churches that were intended to wrest popular support from the Protestants. While its facade is more sober than the Baroque churches put up subsequently, the interior glorifies the new militancy in bronze, gold, marble and precious stones.

Area Sacra Argentina

St Ignatius Loyola, a Spanish soldier who founded the order, has a fittingly magnificent tomb under an altar in the left transept, with a profusion of lapis lazuli, a thin shell fused to plaster stucco.

Just to the south, on the Via delle Botteghe Oscure, is the **Crypta Balbi** (Tue–Sun 9am–7.45pm, June–Sept Fri also 8–10pm), part of the Museo Nazionale Romano. Set on the site of the portico of the Imperial Roman Theatre of Balbus, the museum documents the changing faces of Rome through history.

AROUND THE CAMPO DE' FIORI

The hub of the southern section of the Centro Storico is the **Campo de' Fiori** ⑭, once the site of public executions during the 17th century, now a lively fruit, vegetable and flower market, one of Rome's most attractive and authentic. A reminder of the square's bloody history, however, is provided by the brooding statue of philosopher Giordano Bruno, who was burned alive during the Counter-Reformation in 1600.

Just south of the Campo is another lovely square, Piazza Farnese. Here, the great architects of the age worked on the **Palazzo Farnese** ⓯, Rome's finest Renaissance palace. Begun in 1514 by Antonio da Sangallo the Younger for Cardinal Farnese (Pope Paul III), the project was passed on to Michelangelo, who was responsible for the top floor, and was completed in 1589 by Giacomo della Porta. The building cost so much that it put a great strain on the fortune Farnese had amassed while he was treasurer of the Church. The palace is now the French Embassy, and you need to book a guided tour to see the dining room's mythological frescoes by Annibale Carracci (www.inventerrome. com; Mon and Fri at 5pm, Wed 3pm and 4pm). Facing Palazzo

Market stalls at Campo de' Fiori

Farnese, to the left of the square, is **Palazzo Spada** (www.
gebart.it; Wed–Mon 8.30am–7.30pm), a beautiful example of
Renaissance art, which houses the art collection of Cardinal
Spada in its original setting, including the *trompe l'oeil* trickery
of Borromini's famed Perspective Gallery.

Nearby, housed in an elegant Renaissance mansion, is the
Museo Barracco (Corso Vittorio Emanuele 166/A; www.museo
barracco.it; Tue–Sun Oct–May 10am–4pm Jun–Sept 1–7pm;
free). The museum is devoted to ancient sculpture, not just
from Rome but from Assyria, Egypt, Cyprus, Phoenicia, Etruria
and Greece as well. Highlights of this wonderful collection
include works by the Greek sculptor Polyclitus, engraved marble slabs recovered in the Mesopotamian cities of Nineveh and
Nimrud, and a head of Heracles from Cyprus.

THE JEWISH GHETTO

Retrace your steps to the Campo de' Fiori. The narrow streets
heading southeast of the marketplace take you into the former
Jewish Ghetto, a lively and historic district peppered with restaurants serving the city's distinctive Roman–Jewish cuisine.
Pope Paul IV forced Jews into this confined space in 1555. Rules
were relaxed considerably after his death, but the walls that
confined the quarter were not torn down until 1848. A small
but vibrant Jewish community still lives in and around the Via
del Portico d'Ottavia. The main synagogue sits by the riverbank.
One of the most delightful fountains in Rome, and much loved
by children, is the 16th-century **Fontana delle Tartarughe**
(Turtle Fountain), in Piazza Mattei. It depicts four boys perched
on squirting dolphins while lifting four turtles onto an upper
marble basin, with gracefully outstretched arms.

Nearby is the **Portico d'Ottavia**, a crumbling and arched
facade more than 2,000 years old and dedicated to Augustus'

sister. Beyond it extends the **Teatro di Marcello** ⓰ (Theatre of Marcellus), begun by Julius Caesar, finished under Augustus and said to be the architectural model for the Colosseum.

A short way to the southeast is the little church of **Santa Maria in Cosmedin**, which was given by the Pope to Rome's Greek colony in the 8th century. Its Romanesque facade and simple interior, with beautiful floor mosaics, provide a stark contrast to the city's dominant Baroque grandeur. Test your honesty in the portico's fierce-looking **Bocca della Verità** (Mouth of Truth), made famous by Audrey Hepburn in the 1953 film *Roman Holiday*, on the left wall of the portico. The 12th-century marble face is said to bite off the fingers of anyone putting a hand in the gaping mouth who tells a lie.

Across the road, two of the city's best-preserved temples stand on what was part of the ancient cattle market. The **Tempio Rotondo** ⓱, with its 20 fluted Corinthian columns, was probably dedicated to Hercules and is the oldest standing marble temple in Rome. Its rectangular neighbour, the **Tempio di Fortuna Virile**, is a victim of an ancient typing error, as its presiding deity is believed to have been Portunus, god of harbours, rather than Fortuna (Fortune). A short walk back on the Lungotevere is the imposing **Synagogue** (Lungotevere dei Cenci; www.museoebraico.roma.it; Sun–Thu 10am–6pm, until 5pm in winter, Fri 10am–4pm, until 2pm in winter) built in 1904, housing a museum that traces the history of the Roman Jewish Community.

SPANISH STEPS AND TRIDENTE

The city's most sophisticated shopping district, the area around the **Piazza di Spagna** has been attracting foreigners for centuries. Aristocratic travellers on the Grand Tour came here, as did many of the most celebrated artists of the Romantic era, among them Keats, Byron, Balzac, Wagner and Liszt.

The area continues to attract a cosmopolitan crowd. Well-heeled visitors come for the high-fashion boutiques along Via dei Condotti and its grid of neighbouring cobbled streets. The more casually dressed linger on the glorious and recently restored **Scalinata della Trinità dei Monti**  – the Spanish Steps, named after the nearby residence of the Spanish Ambassador

Fontana della Barcaccia and the Spanish Steps

to the Vatican, the city's most popular meeting place for young Romans and foreigners alike. The steps ascend in three majestic tiers to the 16th-century French church of **Trinità dei Monti**. Its twin belfries and graceful Baroque facade make it one of Rome's most distinctive landmarks. The steps are adorned with pink azaleas in spring, and in summer they make a spectacular location for occasional designer fashion shows.

At the foot of the Spanish Steps lies the **Fontana della Barcaccia**, a fountain in the shape of a sinking boat. The design, attributed to Pietro Bernini or his far more famous son, Gian Lorenzo Bernini, is an ingenious solution to the problem of low pressure in the Acqua Vergine aqueduct at this point, which supplies this fountain (as well as the Trevi Fountain) with water.

The poet John Keats died of consumption in 1821 at the age of 26 in a small room overlooking the Steps. His house, 26 Piazza di Spagna, has since been preserved as the **Keats-Shelley**

Museum (www.keats-shelley-house.org; Mon–Sat 10am–1pm, 2–6pm). On the other side of the Steps, at No. 23, **Babington's Tea Rooms** (www.babingtons.com) is a pleasant old-world bastion of Anglo-Saxon calm and gentility that has been serving tea and scones since the 1890s.

An even more venerable establishment is on nearby Via dei Condotti. **Caffè Greco** (www.anticocaffegreco.eu) has been a favourite haunt of writers and artists ever since it opened in 1760. The autographed portraits, busts and statues attest to its distinguished patrons, among them Casanova, Goethe, Baudelaire, Buffalo Bill, Gogol and Hans Christian Andersen. The thick hot chocolate served here in the winter by frock-coated waiters is a long-standing tradition among stylish Roman shoppers and strollers.

Caffè Greco

VIA DEL CORSO

The **Tridente** area takes its name from the trio of streets built in the 16th century to relieve congestion in Rome's cramped medieval centre. Via del Corso, Via di Ripetta and Via del Babuino emanate like the prongs of a fork from the Piazza del Popolo, for centuries the main entrance to Rome for travellers coming from the north.

The **Via del Corso** is the 1.6km (1-mile) long main street of central Rome, which runs in a straight line from Piazza Venezia to Piazza del Popolo. Known in ancient times as the *Via Lata*, the Corso derives its modern name from the carnival races, or *corse*, that were held here in the 15th century under the spectacle-loving Venetian Pope Paul II. Of all the races, the most thrilling was the *Corsa dei Barberi*, in which riderless Barbary horses, sent into a frenzy by saddles spiked with nails, charged pell-mell along the narrow thoroughfare to be halted at last by a large white sheet hung across the street. Today the partly pedestrianised Corso is lined with palaces and churches and crowded with mainly mid-market large shops, department stores and shoppers. The streets running off it are full of exclusive boutiques, wineries and caffès.

Roughly halfway along the road is the **Piazza Colonna**, where the **column of Marcus Aurelius**, decorated with spiralling reliefs of the Emperor's military triumphs, rises in front of the Italian prime minister's offices in the **Chigi Palace**. The statue of the soldier-emperor that stood on top of the column was replaced in 1589 by one of St Paul.

On the **Piazza di Montecitorio** nearby, dominated by a 6th-century BC Egyptian obelisk, is the **Palazzo Montecitorio**, designed by Bernini for the Ludovisi family. It houses the Camera dei Deputati (Chamber of Deputies), Italy's legislative lower house.

PIAZZA DEL POPOLO

At its northern, pedestrianised end, the Corso culminates in the graceful oval shape of the **Piazza del Popolo** ⑲, a truly exemplary piece of open-air urban theatre, designed in 1818 by Giuseppe Valadier, former architect to Napoleon. The central obelisk, 24-metres (79ft) high, is from the 13th-century BC Egypt of Ramses II. It was brought to Rome by Augustus and erected in the Circus Maximus. Pope Sixtus V had it moved here in 1589.

The square takes its name from the Renaissance church of **Santa Maria del Popolo**, built at the northern gateway to the piazza on the site of Nero's tomb to exorcise his ghost, reputed to haunt the area. In its Baroque interior is a superb fresco of the *Nativity* by the Umbrian painter Pinturicchio in the first chapel on the right, and Raphael's Chigi Chapel, built as a mausoleum for the family of the wealthy Sienese banker and brilliant arts patron, Agostino Chigi. This chapel houses two fine sculptures by Bernini; *Habakkuk* and *Daniel and the Lion*. In the Cerasi Chapel to the left of the altar are two powerful works by Caravaggio, the *Conversion of Saul* and *Crucifixion of St Peter*, notable for the dramatic use of light and shade and the skilful foreshortening of the figures.

The piazza's arched 16th-century **Porta del Popolo** marks the gateway to ancient Rome at the end of the Via Flaminia, which led from Rimini on the Adriatic coast. Pilgrims arriving in Rome by this gate were later greeted by the imposing Baroque churches of Santa Maria dei Miracoli and Santa Maria di Montesanto on the southern side, guarding the entrance to the Corso. Two of the most historic and exclusive caffès in Rome, Rosati and Canova, face each other across the expanse.

PINCIO GARDENS

To the east of the piazza and above the Piazza del Popolo and a monumental complex of terraces, the 19th-century **Pincio Gardens** offer a panoramic view of the piazza and the city, especially at sunset, when the rooftops are tinged with purple and gold. Also the work of Valadier, the statue-populated gardens occupy the site of the 1st-century BC villa of Lucius Licinius Lucullus, a provincial governor who returned enriched by the spoils of Asia and impressed his contemporaries with his extravagant lifestyle. The gardens stretch on to the **Villa Borghese park** (see page 57).

Augustus' Altar of Piece

Lined with pine trees and open-air caffès, the Pincio promenade takes you past **Villa Medici**, built in 1564 and bought by Napoleon in 1803 to house the French Academy in Rome. Today the villa remains home to young French artists visiting the city on scholarships and hosts memorable exhibitions and concerts (www. villamedici.it).

AUGUSTUS' ALTAR OF PEACE

West of the Via del Corso, towards the banks of the River Tiber is the **Ara Pacis Augustae** (www.arapacis.it; daily 9.30am–7.30pm) in Piazza Augusto Imperatore, a fascinating monument, which has been renovated and made into a small museum complex, designed by renowned US architect Richard Meier. After fragments of this 'Altar of Peace', built to celebrate Augustus' victorious campaigns in Gaul and Spain, first came to light in 1568, they were dispersed among several European museums. Most of the pieces were returned to Rome when the building's reconstruction began in the 1930s. The friezes depict Augustus with his wife Livia and daughter Julia, his friend Agrippa and a host of priests and dignitaries. Alongside the altar, the great mound encircled by cypresses is the **Mausoleo di Augusto** (currently closed for restoration), repository of the ashes of the caesars (except Trajan) until Hadrian built his own mausoleum (now the Castel Sant'Angelo see page 61).

Throw a coin

You must throw a coin into the Trevi Fountain, with your right hand over your left shoulder, to ensure a return to Rome. Donations are made to the Red Cross from the collected coins.

THE TREVI FOUNTAIN AND QUIRINALE

The **Fontana di Trevi** ❷⓿ (Trevi Fountain) never fails to astonish. Nicola Salvi's Baroque extravaganza seems a giant stage set, out of all proportion to its tiny piazza. The 18th-century fountain is, in fact, a triumphal arch and palace facade (for the old Palazzo Poli), which frames mythical creatures in a riot of rocks, fountains and pools, all theatrically illuminated at night. The centrepiece is the massive figure of Neptune riding on a seashell drawn by two winged sea horses led by tritons. The rearing horse symbolises the sea's turmoil, the calm steed its tranquillity. Anita Ekberg and Marcello Mastroianni frolicked memorably in the fountain's waters (carried by an ancient Roman aqueduct) when they starred in Federico Fellini's 1960 film *La Dolce Vita* ('The Sweet Life'). Sit on a marble step and enjoy some of the Eternal City's best people-watching.

QUIRINALE

Between Piazza Barberini and the Imperial Forum, and dominating the summit of the highest of the seven hills of ancient Rome, is the Baroque **Palazzo del Quirinale** ❷❶ (www.quirinale.it; Tue–Wed, Fri–Sun, 9.30am–4pm, guided tours only, booking required). This was the summer palace of the popes until the unification of Italy in 1870, when it became home to the new King of Italy. Since 1947, it has been the official residence of the president of the Republic. In the centre of the vast Piazza del Quirinale, magnificent statues of Castor and Pollux and their steeds, all Roman copies of

Greek originals, stand beside an ancient obelisk. Also here is the Scuderie del Quirinale (www.scuderiequirinale.it; opening hours vary), a large space for major exhibitions. The piazza affords a splendid **view** over the whole city towards St Peter's.

Admirers of the Baroque era will find much to delight them in this part of the city, which teems with masterpieces of sculpture and architecture by Bernini. Opposite the *manica lunga* or 'long sleeve' of the Quirinal Palace you will find the small church of **Sant'Andrea al Quirinale**, demonstrating the genius of the 17th-century master in its elliptical plan, gilded dome and stucco work. Further along is the tiny **San Carlo alle Quattro Fontane**, by Bernini's arch-rival, Borromini. It may be small, but with its concave and convex surfaces it is one of Rome's most original church designs.

In the nearby **Piazza Barberini** (at the corner of the Via Veneto) are two of Bernini's celebrated fountains: the **Fontana del Tritone**, which takes centre stage, and the **Fontana delle Api**, on its north side (dedicated to the public and their animals). Both fountains sport the bee symbol taken from the Barberini coat of arms of Pope Urban VIII, Bernini's patron.

The busy genius also had a hand in the architecture of the stately **Palazzo Barberini** 22

The splendid Baroque Trevi Fountain

(1625–33), which now houses part of the **Galleria Nazionale d'Arte Antica** (http://galleriabarberini.beniculturali.it; Tue–Sun 8.30am–7pm; tickets at www.gebart.it). Situated on the Via delle Quattro Fontane, the building provided another architectural battleground for Bernini and rival Borromini, each of whom built one of its grand staircases and contributed to the facade. It is worth a visit as much for its Baroque decor as for its collection of 13th- to 17th-century paintings. Don't forget to look up in the *Salone* or **Great Hall** to see Pietro da Cortona's illusionist ceiling fresco, *Triumph of Divine Providence* (1633–9).

Most of the national art collection is hung in the first-floor gallery (the rest is in the Palazzo Corsini across the Tiber in Trastevere). Works include a Fra Angelico triptych, a portrait of King Henry VIII by Hans Holbein and paintings by Titian, Tintoretto and El Greco. Two stars among many are Raphael's *La Fornarina* ('The Baker's Daughter'), said to be a portrait of

⊙ VIA VENETO

Once the site of a palace surrounded by vast gardens and grounds belonging to the Ludovisi family villa, Via Veneto became renowned in the roaring 1950s and 1960s as the focal point of the so-called *Dolce Vita*, or Hollywood-on-the-Tiber.

This twisting avenue lined with elegant and fashionable caffès became the hangout for the rich and famous stars (Audrey Hepburn, James Stewart, Ingrid Bergman and Marcello Mastroianni) working at Rome's Cinecittà film studios, as well as the less famous hoping to be discovered. Though some of the caffès remain, most of the late 19th-century *palazzi* now house impersonal luxury hotels, offices and tourist-orientated restaurants often with tacky, glass-enclosed outdoor seating.

his mistress and model for many of his madonnas, and Caravaggio's depiction of *Judith Beheading Holofernes*.

From here, Via Barberini leads to Largo Santa Susanna and the church of **Santa Maria della Vittoria**, home to Bernini's *Ecstasy of St Teresa*, a masterpiece of Baroque sculpture.

The Piazza Barberini serves as a base for the Via Veneto (see box), which heads north from here to the park of the Villa Borghese.

Borromini's San Carlo alle Quattro Fontane

VILLA BORGHESE

At the top of Via Veneto, across Piazzale Brasile, is the large and leafy **Villa Borghese** park, once the estate of Cardinal Scipione Borghese, the nephew of Pope Paul V. The Galleria Borghese is in the cardinal's former summer palace; a collection of modern art is in the former Orangery; and Italy's finest Etruscan art collection in the Villa Giulia.

GALLERIA BORGHESE AND MUSEO CARLO BILOTTI

The avid art collector Cardinal Scipione Borghese conceived this handsome Baroque villa on the eastern side of the park as a home for his small but outstanding collection, using his prestige as the nephew of Pope Paul V to acquire coveted masterpieces.

Galleria Borghese ㉓ (http://galleriaborghese.beniculturali.it; Tue–Sun 9am–7pm, entry every two hours; reservation required at www.gebart.it) is one of Italy's best small museums. The principal highlights are some astonishing sculptures by the cardinal's young protégé, Gian Lorenzo Bernini. These include busts of his patron, a vigorous *David* and a graceful sculpture, *Apollo and Daphne*, in which the 26-year-old sculptor depicts the water nymph turning into a laurel just as the god is about to seize her. The gallery's star attraction is Canova's portrayal of Napoleon's sister *Pauline* as a reclining Venus (1805): Pauline married into the Borghese family. Exceptional **paintings** include Raphael's *Deposition*; Titian's *Sacred and Profane Love*; a number of Caravaggio's works, including *David with the Head of Goliath* and the *Madonna of the Serpent*; along with works by Botticelli, Cranach, Dürer and Rubens.

The former Orangery of the Villa Borghese has been transformed into the **Museo Carlo Bilotti** (Viale Fiorello La Guardia; www.museocarlobilotti.it; , Sat–Sun 10am–7pm, June–Sept Tue–Fri 1–7pm, Oct–May Tue–Fri 10am–4pm; free), which houses a precious collection of modern art including the work of de Chirico, Severini, Warhol, and Larry Rivers. Meanwhile, the **Galleria Nazionale d'Arte Moderna e Contemporanea** (National Gallery of Modern and Contemporary Art; http://lagallerianazionale.com; Tue–Sun 8.30am–7.30pm) covers the 1800s to the present and features the work of artists such as Henry Moore, Jackson Pollock, Paul Cézanne and Wassily Kandinsky. Lovers of modern art should visit two more museums: the **MACRO** (www.museomacro.org; Tue–Sun 10.30am–7pm)

Villa Borghese Park

Villa Borghese Park is not only great for a gentle stroll; you can hire bicycles and rollerblades in the grounds, or take a rowing boat out on the picturesque lake.

at Via Nizza 138, with its vast collection of contemporary Italian artists and the **MAXXI** (www.fondazionemaxxi.it; Tue–Fri, Sun 11am–7pm, Sat 11am–10pm), located further north on Via Guido Reni in a beautiful white Zaha Hadid building, dedicated to the great art and photography of the 21st century.

Temple on Villa Borghese's lake

VILLA GIULIA

This 16th-century pleasure palace built for Pope Julius III in the northwest area of the Villa Borghese park, is now the setting for Italy's finest **Etruscan Museum** ❷❹ (Museo Etrusco; www.villagiulia.beniculturali.it; Tue–Sun 8.30am–7.30pm). Although much about this pre-Roman civilisation is still a mystery, the Etruscans (found in Tuscany, Umbria and in parts of Lazio, north of Rome) left a wealth of detail about their customs and everyday life in the personal possessions they buried with their dead. Room after room is filled with objects from the tombs: bronze statues of warriors; shields, weapons and chariots; gold and silver jewellery; decorative vases imported from Greece; and a host of everyday cooking utensils, mirrors and combs.

THE VATICAN

The power of Rome endures both in the spirituality evoked by St Peter's Basilica and in the awe inspired by the splendours of the Vatican City. At their best, the popes and cardinals prevented military conquest through moral leadership and persuasion; at their worst, they could show the same hunger for power and wealth as any caesar or grand duke.

Constantine, the first Christian emperor, erected the original St Peter's Basilica in AD 324, over an oratory on the presumed site of the tomb of the Apostle, who was martyred (with St Paul) in Rome in AD 67. After Saracens sacked it in 846, Pope Leo IV ordered walls to be built around the church, and the enclosed area was known as the Leonine City, and then Vatican City, after the Etruscan name of its location.

The Vatican only became the main residence of the popes after 1378, when the papacy was returned to Rome from exile in Avignon. It has been a sovereign state, independent of Italy, since the Lateran Pact signed with Mussolini in 1929. The Pope is supreme ruler of this tiny state, which is guarded by an elite corps of Swiss Guards, founded in 1506, who still wear the blue, scarlet and orange uniforms said to have been designed by Michelangelo. The papal domain has its own newspaper, L'Osservatore Romano, and a radio station that broadcasts worldwide. It also has shops, banks, a minuscule railway station (rarely used) and an efficient postal service that issues its own Vatican stamps.

Apart from the 1 sq km (0.4 sq miles) comprising St Peter's Square, St Peter's Basilica, and the papal palace and gardens, the Vatican also has jurisdiction over extraterritorial enclaves, including the basilicas of San Giovanni in Laterano, Santa Maria Maggiore and St Paul's, as well as the Pope's summer residence at Castel Gandolfo, to the southeast of the city (www.museivaticani.va).

You don't need a passport to cross the border, though it is marked by a band of white travertine stones running from the ends of the two colonnades at the rim of St Peter's Square. The **Vatican Tourist Information Office** on the south side of

Looking down from the basilica over St Peter's Square

St Peter's Square arranges guided tours and issues tickets to Vatican City, including the gardens. A visit to St Peter's combines well with a tour of Castel Sant'Angelo, but it's best to save the Vatican Museums for a separate day: the 7km (4 miles) of galleries are best savoured in small doses.

CASTEL SANT'ANGELO

Cross the Tiber by the **Ponte Sant'Angelo**, which incorporates arches of Hadrian's original bridge, the Pons Aelius, built in AD 134. The balustrades are adorned with ten angels carved by Bernini and his studio between 1598 and 1660, each bearing a symbol of the Passion of Christ.

From the bridge you have the perfect view of **Castel Sant'Angelo** ㉕ (http://castelsantangelo.beniculturali.it; daily 9am–7.30pm) its mighty brick walls stripped of their travertine cladding and pitted by cannonballs. Conceived by Hadrian as his family mausoleum,

Ponte Sant'Angelo and castle

it became part of the defensive Aurelian Wall a century later. The castle gained its present name in AD 590 after Pope Gregory the Great had a vision of the Archangel Michael alighting on a turret and sheathing his sword to signal the end of a plague. For centuries this was Rome's mightiest military bastion and a refuge for popes in times of trouble; Clement VII holed up here during the sack of Rome by Habsburg troops in 1527.

A spiral ramp, showing traces of the original black-and-white mosaic paving, leads up to the funerary chamber where the ashes of emperors were kept in urns. You emerge into the **Cortile dell'Angelo** (Courtyard of the Angel), which is stacked neatly with cannonballs and watched over by a marble angel. An arms museum opens off the courtyard.

After the grimness of the exterior, it comes as a surprise to step into the luxurious surroundings of the old **Papal Apartments**. Lavish frescoes cover the walls and ceilings of rooms hung with masterpieces by Dosso Dossi, Nicolas Poussin and Lorenzo Lotto. Off the Courtyard of Alexander VI is the most exquisite bathroom in history. Just wide enough for its marble tub, it is painted with delicate designs over every inch of its walls and along the side of the bath.

A harsh jolt brings you back to reality as you enter the **dungeons**, scene of torture and executions. You have to bend over double to get into the bare, stone cells where famous prisoners languished – among them sculptor-goldsmith Benvenuto Cellini and philosopher and monk Giordano Bruno.

The **Gallery of Pius IV**, surrounding the entire building, affords a panoramic view, as does the terrace on the summit, with the 18th-century bronze statue of *St Michael* by Verschaffelt. Opera lovers will recall this as the setting for the final act of Puccini's Tosca, in which the heroine hurls herself to her death from the battlements.

ST PETER'S BASILICA

From Castel Sant'Angelo, a wide, straight avenue, the Via della Conciliazione, leads triumphantly up to St Peter's. A maze of medieval streets, where Raphael had a studio, was destroyed in 1936 by Mussolini's architects to provide an unobstructed view of St Peter's all the way from the banks of the Tiber. A thick wall running parallel to the avenue conceals a passageway (*Il Passetto*), linking the Vatican to the Castel Sant'Angelo for fleeing popes to reach their bastion.

In **Piazza San Pietro** (St Peter's Square), Bernini's greatest creation, is one of the world's most exciting pieces of architectural orchestration. The sweeping curves of the colonnades

⊙ ENTERING ETERNITY

The poet Goethe once said that entering St Peter's is "like entering eternity". The world's largest Roman Catholic church certainly has immense dimensions: 212 metres (695ft) long on the outside, 187 metres (613ft) inside, and 132 metres (433ft) to the tip of the dome. Brass markers on the floor of the central aisle show how far other famous cathedrals fail to measure up.

reach out to embrace Rome and draw pilgrims into the bosom of the Church. On Easter Sunday as many as 300,000 people cram into the piazza to hear Mass. The square is on or near the site of Nero's Circus, where early Christians were martyred.

Bernini completed the 284 travertine columns and 88 pilasters topped by 140 statues of the saints in 11 years, from 1656–67. In the centre rises a 25-metre (82ft) red granite **obelisk**, brought here from Egypt by Caligula in AD 37. Stand on one of the two circular paving stones set between the obelisk and the

⊙ SEEING THE POPE

When he is in Rome, it is possible to see the Pope at his personal residence, the Vatican. He normally holds a public audience every Wednesday at 10.30am in a large modern audience hall (people arrive at 8am for good seats). In summer, the audience is held in St Peter's Square to accommodate the large crowds. In August the papal audience may be held at Castel Gandolfo. An invitation to a papal audience may be obtained from the Prefecture of the Pontifical House by letter (Prefettura della Casa Pontificia, 00120 Città del Vaticano, tel: 06-69885863; www.papalaudience.org – you can download a form from this site) or by going directly to their offices in St Peter's Square the day before between 3pm and 7pm (6pm in winter) or the day of the audience 7am–3pm.

On Sundays at noon, the Pope appears at the window of his apartments in the Apostolic Palace (to the right of the basilica, overlooking the square), delivers a homily, says the Angelus, and blesses the crowd below. On a few major holy days, the pontiff celebrates High Mass in St Peter's and may make an appearance on the basilica's open balcony.

twin 17th-century foun-
tains to see the quadruple
rows of perfectly aligned
Doric columns appear
magically as one.

A grandiose achieve-
ment, **St Peter's Basilica**
㉖ (Basilica di San Pietro;
www.vatican.va; daily 7am–
7pm in summer, 6.30pm in
winter; free; no bare legs
or shoulders) nevertheless
suffers from the compet-
ing visions of its master
architects, who included
Bramante, Carlo Maderno,
Michelangelo and Raphael, each of whom often worked with a
pope peering over his shoulder.

Michelangelo's dome in St Peter's

From 1506, when the new basilica was begun under Julius
II, until 1626 when it was consecrated, St Peter's Basilica
changed form several times. It started out as a simple Greek
cross, with four arms of equal length, as favoured by Bramante
and Michelangelo, and ended up as Maderno's Latin cross,
extended by a long nave, as demanded by the popes of the
Counter-Reformation. One result is that Maderno's porticoed
facade and nave obstruct a clear view of Michelangelo's dome
from the square.

Michelangelo's Masterpiece

The basilica's most worthy artistic treasure, Michelangelo's
Pietà (1500), is in its own chapel to the right of the entrance.
The artist was 25 when he executed this moving marble

sculpture of the Virgin cradling the crucified Christ in her lap. It is the only work that he signed (on the ribbon that crosses the Madonna's breast), after overhearing people crediting it to another sculptor. Since the statue was attacked by a religious fanatic with a hammer in 1972 (the damage was immediately restored), it has been protected by bulletproof glass. Reverence can also cause damage: on the 13th-century bronze statue of St Peter the toes of the right foot have been worn away by the lips and caressing fingers of pilgrims over the centuries.

Beneath the dome, Bernini's great *baldacchino* (canopy) soars over the high altar, at which the Pope celebrates Mass. The canopy and four spiralling columns were cast from bronze beams taken from the Pantheon. At the foot of each column a coat of arms bears the three bees of the Barberini Pope Urban VIII, who commissioned the work. In the apse is another extravagant Baroque work, Bernini's bronze and marble *Cathedra* ('Throne') *of St Peter*, into which the saint's wooden throne is supposedly incorporated. Also by Bernini is the tomb of Urban VIII.

For his imposing **dome** (8am–6pm, 5pm in winter), Michelangelo drew inspiration from the Pantheon and Brunelleschi's cupola on Florence's cathedral. A lift takes you as far as the gallery above the nave, which gives a dizzying view down into the basilica, as well as close-ups of the inside of the dome. A succession of spiral stairs and ramps lead up to the outdoor balcony, which encircles the top of the dome for stunning views of St Peter's Square, the Vatican City and all of Rome.

The **Vatican Grottoes** beneath the basilica contain the tombs of popes and numerous little chapels. The **necropolis**, even deeper underground, shelters pre-Christian tombs, as well as a simple monument that marks St Peter's alleged burial place (Mon–Sat 9am–3.30pm, booking required, email: scavi@fsp. va). Masses are said in the side chapels, in various languages.

THE VATICAN MUSEUMS

It should come as no surprise that the headquarters of the Roman Catholic Church – the world's greatest patron of painters, sculptors and architects – should have one of the world's richest art collections. At the **Vatican Museums** ❷⁷ (Musei Vaticani; www.museivaticani.va; Mon–Sat 9am–6pm, last admission 4pm, free last Sun of the month 9am–2pm, last admission 12.30pm), 7km (4 miles) of rooms and galleries offer a microcosm of Western civilisation. There is a bewildering amount of items to see here.

The fascinating **Museo Pio-Clementino** displays a wonderful collection of classical art salvaged from the ruthless dismantling of ancient monuments in the 16th century to make way for the Renaissance city. The most celebrated piece is the 1st century BC *Laocoön* group: the Trojan priest and his two sons who were strangled by serpents sent by the goddess Athena for refusing to allow the Greek horse to enter Troy. Famous during Imperial times, it was unearthed from a vineyard on the Esquiline Hill in 1506, to the delight of Michelangelo, who rushed to view it. It now stands in a recess of the octagonal Belvedere Courtyard.

Roman copies of some other Greek sculptures, such as the *Aphrodite of*

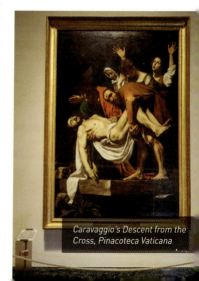

Caravaggio's *Descent from the Cross, Pinacoteca Vaticana*

Cnidos by Praxiteles and the *Apollo Belvedere*, achieved fame as great as the lost originals. In particular, note the powerful, muscular, 1st-century BC *Torso* by Apollonius, which has had a profound influence on artists and sculptors to this day.

The **Museo Etrusco** holds the finds from a 7th-century BC Etruscan burial mound at Cerveteri (see page 87), whose tomb yielded an abundance of treasures. Among the fine jewellery is a gold brooch curiously decorated with lions and ducklings. Look out for the bronze statue of a sprightly Etruscan warrior, the *Mars of Todi*, from the 4th century BC.

Judging by the number of obelisks scattered throughout the city, Egyptian art was much sought after by the ancient Romans. The basis of the collection in the **Museo Egiziano** rests on finds from Rome and its environs, particularly from the Gardens of Sallust between the Pincian and Quirinal hills, the Temple of Isis on the Campus Martius and Hadrian's Villa at Tivoli (see page 83). One room recreates the underground chamber of a tomb in the Valley of the Kings.

The Raphael Rooms

Pope Julius II took a calculated risk in 1508 when he called in a relatively untried 26-year-old to decorate his new residence. The result was the four **Stanze di Raffaello** (the Raphael Rooms). In the central and most visited Stanza della Segnatura are the two masterly frescoes, *Disputation over the Holy Sacrament* and the famous *School of Athens*, which contrasted theological and philosophical wisdom. The *Disputation* unites biblical figures with historical pillars of the faith such as Pope Gregory, Thomas Aquinas and others, including painter Fra Angelico and the divine Dante. At the centre of the *School*, Raphael is believed to have given red-robed Plato the features of Leonardo da Vinci, while portraying Michelangelo as the thoughtful Heraclitus, seated in the foreground. Raphael himself appears in the lower right-hand corner.

For a stark contrast to Raphael's grand manner, seek out the gentle beauty of Fra Angelico's frescoes in the **Cappella del Beato Angelico** (Chapel of Nicholas V). The lives of saints Lawrence and Stephen are told in delicately subdued pinks and blues, highlighted with gold.

Giuseppe Momo's staircase

The six richly decorated halls of the **Borgia Apartments** contain Pinturicchio's frescoes, with portraits of the Spanish Borgia Pope Alexander VI, and leads into the **Collection of Modern Religious Art** opened in 1973 by Paul VI. Among the 20th-century works are Matisse's Madonna sketches, Rodin bronzes, Picasso ceramics, designs for ecclesiastical robes and, somewhat unexpectedly, a grotesque pope by Francis Bacon.

One of Europe's finest collections of ancient manuscripts and rare books is held in the **Apostolic Library**. In the great reading room, or Sistine Hall, designed by Domenico Fontana in 1588, walls and ceilings are covered with paintings of ancient libraries, conclaves, thinkers and writers. Showcases holding precious manuscripts have replaced the old lecterns. A 1,600-year-old copy of Virgil's works, the poems of Petrarch, a 6th-century gospel of St Matthew and Henry VIII's love letters to Anne Boleyn are among the prized possessions.

The sumptuous Sistine Chapel

The Sistine Chapel

Nothing can prepare you for the shock of the **Sistine Chapel** (Cappella Sistina), built for Sixtus IV in the 15th century. Restored in a 20-year project that finished in 1994, the brightness and freshness of the frescoes are overwhelming. At the time some art critics claimed that the frescoes had been cleaned beyond recognition and had lost their original tonality. Be that as it may, visitors seem to yield to the power of Michelangelo's ceiling and his *Last Judgement*. The other wall frescoes, by Botticelli, Ghirlandaio, Pinturicchio, Rosselli and Signorelli, are barely acknowledged. In this private papal chapel, where cardinals hold their conclaves to elect new popes, the glory of the Catholic Church achieves its finest artistic expression.

The chapel portrays the biblical story of man, in three parts: from Adam to Noah; the giving of the Law to Moses; and from the birth of Jesus to the Last Judgement. Towards the centre of the ceiling you will be able to make out the celebrated out-stretched finger of the *Creation of Adam*. Most overwhelming of all is the impression of the whole. This is best appreciated looking back from the bench by the chapel's exit.

On the chapel's altar wall is Michelangelo's tempestuous *Last Judgement*, finished 25 years after the ceiling's completion in 1512, when the artist was in his sixties. An almost naked Jesus dispenses justice; he is more like a stern, classical god-hero than the conventionally gentle biblical figure. It is said that the artist's agonising self-portrait can be seen in the flayed skin of St Bartholomew, below Jesus.

The Picture Gallery

Amid all the Vatican's treasures, the 15 rooms of the **Pinacoteca Vaticana** (Picture Gallery) in a separate wing, sometimes get short shrift. Covering nine centuries of painting, there are important works by Fra Angelico, Perugino, Raphael's *Transfiguration*, Leonardo da Vinci's unfinished *St Jerome*, Bellini's *Pietà* and Caravaggio's *Descent from the Cross*. As you wander the galleries, glance out of the windows to view St Peter's dome over the Vatican Gardens (the best views are from the Gallery of the Maps). Take a rest in the Cortile della Pigna, dominated by the bronze pine-cone fountain (1st century AD) which gives the courtyard its name.

TRASTEVERE, THE AVENTINE & TESTACCIO

The Ponte Fabricio, one of Rome's oldest bridges (62 BC), links the left bank to the tiny **Isola Tiberina** (Tiber Island). Three centuries before Christ the island was the sacred property of Aesculapius, god of healing, to whom a temple and hospital were dedicated. The large **Fatebenefratelli** hospital, originally founded in 1548 by the friars of St John of God, stands here to this day, occupying most of the island. A second bridge, Ponte Cestio, remodelled in the 19th century, leads over to the river's right bank and the neighbourhood of Trastevere.

TRASTEVERE

Trastevere, 'across the Tevere (Tiber)', has been Rome's traditional working-class quarter since ancient times, and its inhabitants pride themselves on being the true Romans. Despite gentrification that has dotted the district with smart shops and eateries, Trastevere retains a lively character all of its own, particularly in the cobbled streets around Piazza di Santa Maria in Trastevere. The church of **Santa Maria in Trastevere** ⓲ is reputedly the oldest in the city. Its foundation can be traced to the 3rd century AD, but the present structure dates from 1130–43 and is the work of Pope Innocent II, himself a *Trasteverino*. The facade is decorated with a beautiful 13th-century mosaic of the Virgin flanked by 10 maidens bearing lamps. The highlights of the interior are undoubtedly the 12th-century Byzantine mosaics covering the floor and apse.

Before entering **Santa Cecilia in Trastevere**, pause in the courtyard of the church to admire the russet Baroque facade and endearingly leaning Romanesque tower (AD 1113). Now regarded as the patron saint of music, St Cecilia was martyred for her Christian faith in AD 230. Her chapel stands over the site of her home and caldarium (the bathhouse, still visible), in which she was tortured

'We others'

Noantri, dialect for 'we others', reflects the way the Trasteverini see themselves. It is also the name of their festival of music, food and fireworks in the last two weeks of July.

by scalding and finally beheaded. The sculptor Stefano Maderno was on hand when her tomb was excavated in 1599 and his beautiful statue shows the miraculously conserved body that served as his model.

The **Museo di Roma in Trastevere** (www.museodi romaintrastevere.it; Tue–Sun 10am–8pm) is housed in a former Carmelite convent on Piazza di Sant'-Egidio. A series of life-sized

Santa Maria in Trastevere apse

exhibits including a chemist and an inn represent the daily life of 19th-century Rome, and paintings, prints, drawings and watercolours reveal the changing face of the city and surrounding countryside, as seen by local and visiting artists.

The **Gianicolo** (Janiculum Hill) can be reached from Trastevere by following the long and winding Via Garibaldi uphill. After the liberation of Rome from papal rule in 1870, this hill became a gathering place where anticlerical citizens could honour Giuseppe Garibaldi. A large equestrian monument to the freedom-fighter stands on **Piazzale Garibaldi** ㉙ and, a little further north, is another for his wife, the intrepid Anita. The **views** from the terrace are magnificent. Also on the hill is **San Pietro in Montorio**, which contains works by Vasari, del Piombo and Bernini. Bramante's tiny **Tempietto**, one of the gems of the Renaissance, was erected in the courtyard in 1502.

The Tempietto

Bramante's Tempietto is one of the finest examples of High Renaissance architecture. Set in an Early Renaissance courtyard, it possesses a gravity all of its own – marking the alleged site of St Peter's crucifixion.

THE AVENTINE

Revered in ancient times as the 'Sacred Mount', when it stood outside Rome's walls, the Aventine Hill (Monte Aventino) remains a quiet sanctuary above the clamour of the city. An aristocratic district in the Imperial era, the hill is still a favoured residential zone, with villas and apartments set in shady gardens.

The Aventine is also the site of some of the earliest Christian churches, the most beautiful of which is the basilica of **Santa Sabina 30**, built around AD 425. The 24 white Corinthian columns lining the nave give the church a classic harmony, while the beautiful carved 5th-century cypress-wood doors in the portico contain one of the earliest depictions of the crucifixion. Through an atrium window you can see a descendant of an orange tree planted by St Dominic in 1220. A few steps away stands the villa of the **Cavalieri di Malta** (Knights of Malta). Peep through the keyhole of the closed garden gates for a perfectly framed view of the dome of the distant St Peter's.

TESTACCIO

Just below the genteel residential slopes of the Aventine Hill lies the bustling neighbourhood of **Testaccio**, traditionally working-class and now on the rise. The Mattatoio was a slaughterhouse until 1975. These days, part of the complex hosts a (somewhat distant) wing of the MACRO contemporary art museum; technically called MACRO Testaccio, but commonly referred to as MACRO Mattatoio (www.museomacro.org; open during exhibitions only, Tue–Sun 2–8pm). Prestigious international exhibitions – including some massive installations – take advantage of this unusual exhibition space. There's a busy nightlife scene in Testaccio, with some of the most authentic *trattorie* in Rome and a growing array of chic wine bars and delis.

For something more tranquil, head to Porta San Paolo, where dark cypresses shade the beautiful **Cimitero Acattolico** ③ (Protestant Cemetery; www.cemeteryrome.it; Mon–Sat 9am–5pm, Sun 9am–12.30pm), where John Keats was buried in 1821 and where the ashes of his friend Shelley were interred the following year. Towering over the cemetery is Rome's only **pyramid** (Piramide di Caio Cestio), which has survived because it was incorporated in the city walls. A colonial magistrate, Caius Cestius, commissioned the 30-metre (100ft) monument for his tomb in 20 BC on his return from Egypt.

MONTI AND ESQUILINO

On the western side of the Esquiline Hill lies the large *rione* (neighbourhood) of **Monti**, encompassing the Fori Imperiali and two major basilicas: Santa Maria Maggiore and San Giovanni in Laterano. In the hilly, leafy streets between Via Panisperna and Via Cavour, it has retained interesting traces of its medieval past,

Sculpture of Saint Cecilia in Santa Cecilia in Trastevere

Niobid statue, Palazzo Massimo

as well as an intimate village feel. On the other side of the hill is Piazza Vittorio Emanuele II, the focal point of the **Esquilino** rione, a truly multi-ethnic area, with many international food shops and an interesting market selling fresh produce, spices, clothes and domestic goods on Via Lamarmora.

DIOCLETIAN'S BATHS AND PALAZZO MASSIMO

Part of the Museo Nazionale Romano, the **Terme di Diocleziano** ③② (Tue–Sun 9am–7.30pm, in summer also Fri 8–11pm) offer a good introduction to Rome's Greek and Roman antiquities. Larger even than those of Caracalla, Diocletian's Baths covered 120 hectares (300 acres), part of which are now occupied by the Piazza della Repubblica and the church of Santa Maria degli Angeli, near the Termini station.

The largest part of the Museo Nazionale Romano collection is housed in the nearby 19th-century **Palazzo Massimo** (www.coopculture.it; Tue–Sun 9am–7.45pm, in summer also Fri 8–11pm), including frescoes taken from the imperial villa of Livia. These show nature at its most bountiful, with flowers, trees, birds and fruit painted with great attention to detail (visited only as part of a guided tour). There is also an impressive collection of statues and busts of emperors, their relatives and lovers, and mythological creatures. Highlights include the

Niobid statue from the Gardens of Sallust, the seated bronze *Pugilist* or Boxer, and the *Sleeping Hermaphroditus*. There are also collections of ancient Roman jewellery, as well as coins from the Republic and Imperial eras up until the Renaissance.

SANTA MARIA MAGGIORE

Southeast of the Piazza della Repubblica is the Basilica of **Santa Maria Maggiore ③**. According to a 13th-century legend, this largest and most splendid of all the churches dedicated to the Virgin Mary was built in the 4th century by Pope Liberius after a vision from the Virgin Mary. In fact, the church almost certainly dates from AD 420, and was completed soon afterwards by Pope Sixtus III.

Glittering **mosaics** enhance the perfect proportions of the interior. Above the 40 ancient Ionic columns of the triple nave, a mosaic frieze portrays Old Testament scenes leading to the coming of Christ. The theme is continued in the gilded Byzantine-style mosaics on the triumphal arch, detailing the birth and the childhood of Jesus, and culminates in the magnificent 13th-century portrayal of Mary and Jesus enthroned in the apse behind the high altar. Inlaid red and green precious marbles pattern the floor in a style pioneered by Rome's illustrious Cosmati family of craftsmen during the 12th century.

Just south of Via Cavour is the 5th-century **San Pietro in Vincoli ③**, built as a sanctuary for the chains with which Herod bound St Peter in Palestine. It contains one of Michelangelo's greatest sculptures, *Moses*, which was intended for St Peter's as part of the sculptor's unsuccessful project for Julius II's tomb. Moses was going to be just one of 40 figures adorning the tomb, but the plan was aborted when Julius decided he wanted Michelangelo to paint the Sistine Chapel instead.

SAN GIOVANNI IN LATERANO

Situated in a large piazza to the southeast of the Colosseum is the mother church of the Roman Catholic world (seat of the Pope as Bishop of Rome), **San Giovanni in Laterano** ㉟, which predated the first St Peter's Basilica by a few years. Popes lived in the Lateran Palace for 1,000 years until they moved to Avignon, and then to the Vatican on their return in 1377.

Fire, earthquake and looting by Vandals reduced the church to ruins over the centuries. The present structure uses the bronze central doors that once graced the entrance to the Curia in the Forum in ancient Rome. High above the basilica's facade, 15 giant white statues of Jesus, John the Baptist and Church sages stand against the sky.

Transformed by Borromini in the 17th century, the sombre interior is more restrained than is usual for Baroque architects. The only exuberant touches are the coloured marble inlays of the paving and statues of the Apostles. The **baptistery**, site of the first Christian baptism in Rome, preserves some 5th- to 7th-century mosaics. Brothers Jacopo and Pietro Vassalletto excelled themselves in the **cloisters**, where alternating straight and twisted columns, in mosaic style, are a perfect setting for meditation.

The Basilica of San Clemente

An ancient edifice opposite the basilica – almost all that's left of the original Lateran Palace – shelters the **Scala Santa**, the stairway brought back by St Helena from Jerusalem and said to have been trodden by Jesus in the house of Pontius Pilate. The devout still climb the 28 marble steps to the **Sancta Sanctorum** ('Holy of Holies', the private chapel of the popes; charge) on their knees.

Ancient obelisk

Outside San Giovanni in Laterano stands an obelisk brought from the Temple of Ammon in Thebes. It is the tallest in the world – 32 metres (102ft) – and, dating from the 15th century BC, very possibly the oldest of the 13 still standing in Rome.

SAN CLEMENTE

On the Via San Giovanni in Laterano stands a gem of a church, which hides a fascinating history within its three levels. In its present basilica form, **San Clemente** ❸ dates from the 12th century, with three naves divided by ancient columns and embellished by a pavement of geometric designs. A symbolic mosaic in the apse features the Cross as the Tree of Life nourishing all living things: birds, animals and plants. To the right of the nave, a staircase leads down to the 4th-century **basilica**, which underpins the present church. The Romanesque frescoes, unfortunately, have drastically faded, but copies show the near-perfect condition in which they were uncovered early in the 20th century.

An ancient stairway leads deeper underground to a maze of corridors and chambers, believed to be the home of St Clement himself, third successor to St Peter as Pope and martyred by Hadrian in AD 88. Also here is the earliest religious structure on the site, a 2nd-century AD pagan **temple** (*Mithraeum*) dedicated to the god Mithras.

The Old Appian Way

FURTHER AFIELD

VIA APPIA ANTICA

Don't miss a visit to the **Via Appia Antica** ㊲, the Old Appian Way, just outside the city walls. Heading southeast through the Porta San Sebastiano, look back for a good view of the old **Aurelian Wall**, still enclosing part of Rome. Its massive defensive ramparts stretch into the distance, topped by towers and bastions built to resist the onslaught of Barbarian invasions in the 3rd century. Ahead lies a narrow lane, hemmed in at first by hedges and the high walls of film stars' and millionaires' homes – the Old Appian Way. When the Censor Appius Claudius opened the consular road and gave it his name in 312 BC, the Appian Way was the first of the great Roman roads. You can still see some of the original paving stones over which the Roman legions marched 370km (222 miles) on their way to Brindisi to set sail for the Levant and North Africa.

By law, burials could not take place within the city walls, so on either side of the road lie the ruins of sepulchres of 20 generations of patrician Roman families, some with simple tablets, others with impressive mausoleums.

At a fork in the road, the 17th-century chapel of **Domine Quo Vadis** marks the spot where St Peter, fleeing Nero's persecution, is said to have met Christ and asked: *'Domine, quo vadis?'*

('Whither goest thou, Lord?'). Christ is believed to have replied: 'I go to Rome to be crucified again.' Ashamed of his fear, Peter turned back to Rome and his own crucifixion.

THE CATACOMBS

Further along the Appia Antica, within a short distance of each other, are three of Rome's most celebrated **catacombs**: Domitilla, San Callisto (the largest and the most famous) and San Sebastiano. Millions of early Christians, among them many martyrs and saints, were buried in 50 of these vast underground cemeteries. Guides accompany groups into a labyrinth of damp, musty-smelling tunnels and chambers burrowed into the soft volcanic tufa rock, sometimes six levels deep. Early Christian paintings and carvings adorn the catacombs.

The **Catacombs of Domitilla** are the oldest and perhaps the most enjoyable to visit (www.domitilla.info; daily 9am–noon, 2–5pm, closed mid-Dec–mid-Jan). These are the most extensive catacombs, and the only ones still to contain bones, and have the additional attraction of an entrance that goes through a sunken 4th-century church. The entrance to the **Catacombs of San Callisto** lies at the end of an avenue of cypresses (www.catacombe.roma.it; daily 9am–noon, 2–5pm, closed all Feb). An official tour takes you down to the second level of excavations, where you will see the burial niches, or *loculi*, cut into the rock one above the other on either side of the dark galleries. Occasionally the narrow passages open out into larger chambers, or *cubicula*, where a family would be buried together. More than 10 early popes were buried here. In the **Catacombs of San Sebastiano** (www.catacombe.org; Mon–Sat 10am–5pm, closed Dec), the bodies of the apostles Peter and Paul are said to have been hidden during the 3rd-century persecutions.

Near the Catacombs of San Callisto is the poignant memorial of **Fosse Ardeatine**, which has become a place of pilgrimage for modern Italians. In March 1944, in retaliation for the killing of 32 German soldiers by the Italian Resistance, the Nazis rounded up at random 335 Italian men (10 for each German and an extra 15 for good measure) and machine-gunned them in the sandpits of the Via Ardeatina.

The cylindrical **Tomb of Cecilia Metella** (www.coopculture. it; Tue–Sat 9am–1 hour before sunset) dominates the Appian landscape. This noblewoman was the wife of the immensely rich Crassus, who financed Julius Caesar's early campaigns. The well-preserved **Circus of Maxentius**, built for chariot races in AD 309, extends alongside.

Further south (entrance at Via Appia Nuova 1092) is the 2nd-century **Villa dei Quintili** (www.coopculture.it; Tue–Sun 9am–1 hour before sunset), the Quintili brothers' sumptuous residence, with a bath complex and nymphaeum, and the **Parco degli Acquedotti**, dotted with the remains of Roman aqueducts.

OSTIENSE

South of Testaccio lie the Ostiense and Garbatella quarters, filled with striking late 19th- and early 20th-century workers' apartment blocks. Once industrial, Ostiense is becoming more gentrified, offering some of Rome's hippest nightlife.

In a former electricity power plant, a 10-minute walk from Testaccio's pyramid, is one of Rome's must-see sights for all ages. The **Centrale Montemartini** (Via Ostiense 106; www.centralemontemartini.org; Tue–Sun, 9am–7pm) has been converted into a fascinating museum that juxtaposes industrial machinery with more than 400 classic Roman statues.

Between Via Guglielmo Marconi and the Tiber lies **San Paolo Fuori le Mura**. Originally built by Constantine in AD 314 and enlarged by Valentinian II and Theodosius, St Paul's was Rome's largest church after St Peter's. It stood intact until razed by fire in 1823, but was faithfully restored.

Massive Byzantine doors in 11th-century bronze panels survived the fire and now appear on the west wall. A **ciborium** (1285) attributed to the Florentine architect and sculptor Arnolfo di Cambio decorates the high altar, under which lies the supposed burial place of St Paul the Apostle.

The Circus of Maxentius

Above the 86 Venetian marble columns runs a row of mosaic medallions representing all the popes, from St Peter to the present day. A main feature is the peaceful Benedictine cloister from the early 13th century.

EXCURSIONS

TIVOLI AND THE SABINE HILLS

The picturesque town of **Tivoli** perches on a steep slope amid the **Sabine Hills**. Inhabited even in ancient times, when it was known as *Tibur*, Tivoli prospered throughout the Middle Ages. It preserves interesting Roman remains, as well as medieval churches and its famous Renaissance villa. Cotral buses (www.cotralspa. it) connect Rome to Tivoli from the Ponte Mammolo metro station

A 'Third Rome'?

Beyond the ancient and modern city, a 'Third Rome' exists 5km (3 miles) south along the Ostian Way. A complex of massive white-marble buildings, EUR was designed for a world fair in 1942 to mark 20 years of Fascism. War halted con-struction, and the fair never took place. EUR is now a thriving township of govern-ment ministries, offices and an array of museums including the Museum of Roman Civilization (www. museociviltaromana.it).

(line B). Not all the buses stop at Villa Adriana. By car, the drive takes 45 minutes on Via Tiburtina; or take the A4 Autostrada towards Aquila and exit at Tivoli.

Villa d'Este, Villa Adriana and Villa Gregoriana

The **Villa d'Este** ⊛ (www. villadestetivoli.info; Tue-Sun 8.30am–1 hour before sunset, in summer Fri–Sat also 8pm–midnight) sprawls along the hillside. From its balconies you can survey its fabled gardens, which fall away in a series of terraces – a paradise of cypresses, umbrella pines, fountains (some 500) and statues. Card-inal Ippolito II d'Este conceived this modest villa and garden in 1550; architect Piero Ligorio created it. On the **Viale delle Cento Fontane** water jets splash into a basin guarded by statues of eagles. The **Fontana dell'Organo**, originally accompanied by organ music, cascades steeply down the rocks.

5km (3 miles) down the road, tucked away at the foot of the hills, lie the ruins of **Villa Adriana** ⊛ (Hadrian's Villa; www.coopculture. it; daily 9am–1 hour before sunset). Spread over 70 hectares (173 acres), this retirement hideaway of the Emperor Hadrian was one of the most extravagant of such projects in ancient times. You enter the ruins through the colonnades of the Greek-style **Pecile** (a pool which was once surrounded by a portico), which leads to the imperial residence. Adjoining the palace are guest rooms, their mosaic floors visible, and an underground passage-way through which servants moved about. The **Teatro Marittimo**, a pavilion surrounded by a reflecting pool and circular portico, epit-omises the magic of the place. To the south, remnants of arches and copies of Greek-style caryatids surround the **Pool of Canopus** leading to the sanctuary of the Egyptian god Serapis.

Villa Gregoriana (www.visitfai.it/parcovillagregoriana; Tue–Sun 10am–6.30pm, until 4pm in winter; closed Jan and Feb), in the centre of Tivoli, is an oasis of waterfalls, ravines and grottoes. In 1826 the River Aniene burst its banks and swept away much of the town. Architect Clemente Folchi duly diverted the river, boring into the mountainside to create a series of spectacular waterfalls. Colour-coded walks lead off from the main waterfall, ending up

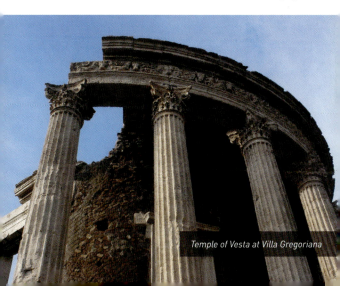

Temple of Vesta at Villa Gregoriana

Floor mosaic at Ostia

at the **Temple of Vesta**, a round, travertine structure dating back to the 1st century BC.

OSTIA ANTICA

Excavations continue to uncover fascinating sections of what was once the seaport and naval base of Rome when it was the most important city in the Western world. The long-buried city of Ostia stands at the mouth (*ostium*) of the Tiber, 23km (14 miles) southwest of the capital on the shores of the Tyrrhenian Sea. Sea-going vessels were unable to travel inland along the shallow Tiber, so river barges plied back and forth from the port, carrying imperial Rome's supply of food and building materials. During its heyday, the port city had 100,000 residents, two splendid public baths, a theatre (where plays are still occasionally offered), many temples and wealthy villas.

The ruins of **Ostia Antica**  (www.ostiaantica.beniculturali.it; Apr–Aug Tue–Sun 8.30am–7.15pm, Sept until 7pm, Oct 6.30pm, Nov–mid-Feb 4.30pm, mid Feb–Mar 5pm), set among cypresses and pines (perfect for picnics), may reveal more about daily life and the building methods of ancient Rome than do those of the capital. Excavations since the 19th century have unearthed **Decumanus Maximus** (Main Street) and a grid of side streets.

The **Piazzale delle Corporazioni** (Square of the Guilds) housed 70 commercial offices around a porticoed central temple to Ceres, goddess of agriculture. Mosaic mottoes and emblems in the pavement tell of the trading of grain factors, caulkers, ropemakers and shipowners from all over the world. The **theatre** next door is worth the climb up the tiered seats for a view over the whole ruined city.

As in Rome, the **Forum** was the focus of city life, dominated at one end by the Capitol, a temple dedicated to Jupiter, Juno and Minerva, and at the other by the Temple of Rome and Augustus, with the Curia (seat of the municipal authorities) and the basilica, or law courts, lying in between.

To see a typical residence, visit the **House of Cupid and Psyche** with its rooms paved in marble and built round a central garden courtyard. Nearby a small on-site museum traces Ostia's history through statues, busts and frescoes.

The 1930s resort of **Lido di Ostia** attracts weekending Romans. The sea is not very clean here, but it is lined with *stabilimenti* (beach clubs), many of which have restaurants and pools. There are some sections of *spiaggia libera* ('free beach', without a fee) and at night bars open up on the beach.

CERVETERI

The **Etruscan necropolis** at **Cerveteri** ❹, 43km (27 miles) northwest of Rome, was known as *Caere*, one of the 12 towns of the powerful Etruscan League, which declined in the 3rd century BC after becoming a Roman dependency (www.tarquinia-cerveteri.it; Tue–Sun 8.30am–until dusk). The scores of **tombs** here represent every kind of burial, dating from the 7th to 1st century BC. Decorations and carvings depict the things that Etruscans felt they needed in the afterlife. The **Museo Nazionale Cerite**, housed in a 16th-century castle in Piazza Santa Maria, displays a collection of objects from the tombs (Tue–Sun 8.30am–7.30pm).

BVLGARI

10

Upmarket shopping in Via Condotti

WHAT TO DO

SHOPPING

Italian fashions and artisan products are extremely popular and it's not unusual to buy a suitcase to take home some goodies. The small, traditional shops are fun to browse and real bargains can be found in the January and July sales.

IVA (value-added tax) is incorporated into prices on a sliding scale, reaching 22 percent. Non-EU citizens are entitled to a refund of this tax on purchases of €155 or more, if made in one place; ask for an invoice from the seller. Save receipts until you leave your last EU destination. If you are leaving from Rome, take your receipts to be stamped before you check in. For more information, visit www.globalblue.com.

WHERE TO SHOP

The most fashionable (and expensive) shopping district lies between Piazza di Spagna and Via del Corso. The best in high fashion, jewellery, fabrics and leather is available in elegant shops on Via dei Condotti and its side streets: Via Borgognona, Via Frattina and Via Bocca di Leone. Stroll from Piazza di Spagna to Piazza del Popolo on Via del Babuino for other famous-name boutiques. Streets branching from Campo de' Fiori are good for quirky fashion and artisans' boutiques and workshops.

Via Cola di Rienzo, just across the river, is not so exclusive but its stores offer good and sometimes excellent quality. Via Nazionale and Via del Tritone are less expensive places for clothes and leather.

The best of Rome's few big stores are Coin (Piazzale Appio, near San Giovanni in Laterano and Termini Station) and

La Rinascente (inside the Galleria Alberto Sordi on Piazza Colonna and another branch on Piazza Fiume). The Oviesse and Upim chains are good for essentials.

Be prepared to haggle at Porta Portese, Rome's famous flea market held on Sunday morning in tiny streets parallel to Viale Trastevere between Porta Portese and Piazza Ippolito Nievo in Trastevere. You will find clothes, furniture, bric-a-brac, jewellery and books.

The outdoor market in Via Sannio (near San Giovanni in Laterano) has bargain clothes (Mon–Sat 8.30am–1.30pm). Between Via G. Pepe and Via Mamiani, in former barracks, is Nuovo Mercato Esquilino, Rome's colourful and multicultural food and clothes market.

WHAT TO BUY

Antiques. Dealers by the score sell exquisite (but expensive) silver, glass, porcelain, furniture and paintings. The best shops are on Via del Babuino and Via Margutta (between the Spanish Steps and the Piazza del Popolo), Via Giulia (behind Palazzo Farnese) and Via dei Coronari (near Piazza Navona). Buy only from a reputable dealer, who will provide a certificate of guarantee and obtain a government export permit.

Books and prints. The open-air market at Largo Fontanella Borghese (off Via del Corso, Mon–Sat 9am–7pm) specialises in prints and books.

Ceramics. Leone Limentani (Via del Portico d'Ottavia 47; www.limentani.com) has a wealth of ceramics, with discounts on discontinued lines.

Fashion. All the famous names of Italian *alta moda* (high fashion) are represented in the Piazza di Spagna area. Fendi and Valentino are Rome's local stars, but you'll find all their peers as well:

Armani, Etro, Krizia, Prada, Missoni, Versace, Gucci and Max Mara.

Food and wine. Delicacies include Parmesan, salami, Parma and San Daniele ham (*prosciutto crudo* – meat products cannot be taken to the US), extra virgin olive oil, Castelli Romani wines and fiery *grappa*. Ai Monasteri in Corso Rinascimento (off Piazza Navona; http://aimonasteri.it) sells liqueurs, confectionery, olive oil and other products

Street stalls

made by Italian monasteries. Trimani (Via Goito 20; www.trimani.com) is the city's most historic wine shop (since 1821).

Interior design. Showrooms worth visiting include Magazzini Associati (Passeggiata di Ripetta; www.magazziniassociati.it), a modern design store offering contemporary furniture and Atelier Monti (Via Panisperna 42; www.ateliermonti.it) close to the Colosseum. For the latest in lighting head for Artemide (Via Pisanelli 1; www.artemide.it) and Flos (Via del Babuino 84; www.flos.com).

Jewellery. You'll find modern, antique and costume jewellery. Bulgari in Via dei Condotti for opulence, or the stores on Via del Governo Vecchio – particularly Tempi Moderni (No. 108) – for vintage and costume jewellery.

Leather. Stylish shoes, handbags, gloves, wallets and luggage abound. Furla (www.furla.com), on Piazza di Spagna, sells fashionable and affordable bags.

ENTERTAINMENT

Rome offers a wealth of evening entertainment, especially in summer when balmy evenings entice everyone outdoors. Rome's summer festival, the *Estate Romana* (www.estate romana.comune.roma.it), runs from June to September and offers music, film, dance and theatre in venues across the city.

MUSIC VENUES

The best venue for **classical and contemporary music** is the Auditorium Parco della Musica (Viale Pietro de Coubertin 30, tel: 06-80241281, www. auditorium.com), with a large outdoor amphitheatre, three indoor halls and exhibition spaces. Bus 910 runs from Stazione Termini to the Auditorium. The renowned Accademia di Santa Cecilia (www.santacecilia.it) and its symphonic and chamber orchestras host their main concerts at the Auditorium from October to May. Classical music is also performed in historic settings, such as the Campidoglio (see page 28), the beautifully frescoed Oratorio del Gonfalone and the cloister of Santa Maria della Pace. Outdoor venues include Villa Ada,

La Traviata

Teatro di Marcello and Villa Celimontana.

Opera and ballet performances are presented at the Teatro dell'Opera (Piazza Beniamino Gigli near Via Torino, tel: 06-481601, www.opera roma.it). The opera season runs from November to late spring, with ballet the rest of the year. In July and August the troupe perform a selection of operas and ballets outdoors in the highly evocative Baths of Caracalla.

Out clubbing

Music clubs abound, from jazz, blues and folk to rock, reggae and salsa. Major live venues are Atlantico Live (Viale dell'Oceano Atlantico 271D, tel: 06-591 5727, www.atlan ticoroma.it), Locanda Atlantide (Via dei Lucani 22/B, tel: 06-96045875, www.locandatlantide.it) and Circolo degli Artisti (Via Casilina Vecchia 42, tel: 320 872 0366). Blues and jazz are found at Trastevere's Big Mama (Vicolo San Francesco a Ripa 18, tel: 06-5812551, www.bigmama.it), Alexanderplatz (Via Ostia 9, tel: 320 332 3236; www.alexanderplatzjazzclub.it), and Casa del Jazz (Via di Porta Ardeatina, 55, tel: 06-704731, www. casajazz.it).

Cinemas usually show foreign films in Italian. Exception is the Nuovo Olimpia (near the Spanish Steps; http://nuovo olimpia.ccroma.circuitocinema.com). Look for the 'V.O.' (versione originale) label on a local paper's movie listings.

NIGHTLIFE

Nightlife in Rome used to be limited to the **Testaccio** club hub on the south side of town near Piramide. The area continues to expand, stretching toward **Via Ostiense**, and attracts a varied, if mostly younger crowd. The modern suburb of **EUR** also has popular nightclubs with visiting DJs. In the summer, the beach clubs in **Ostia** morph into dance clubs, often offering live music. The **Centre** is more about wine bars and sophisticated clientele.

Spazio 900 in EUR (Viale Marconi 5, www.spazionovecento.it) is a bastion for special events and fancy dancers: DJs from Ibiza frequently moonlight here. **La Saponeria** in Ostiense (Via Degli Argonauti 20, Friday and Saturday night) is a packed-to-the-gills dance club featuring hip-hop and house music. Nearby, the famous DJs at **Goa** (Via Libetta 13, www.goaclub.com) keep locals up until dawn with electro and house beats. **Micca Club** near Porta Maggiore (Via Pietro Micca 7a, www.miccaclub.com) is the place for burlesque, live jazz, DJ sets until late, and great aperitivos. A very hip hangout is **Caffé Propaganda** (Via Claudia, 15, www.caffepropaganda.it), serving great drinks to a cosmopolitan crowd in a sumptuous turn-of-the-century interior.

In Trastevere, **Friends** (Piazza Trilussa 41, www.cafefriends. it) is a trendy, modern bar on crowded Piazza Trilussa. The drinks are great, and this is the perfect starting point for a night out in the area. Other hip bars include **Doney** (Via Veneto 141; www.restaurantdoney.com/it), a 1960s era Dolce Vita cocktail bar that has had a number of facelifts and still attracts a dashing crowd. Lively **Bartaruga** in the Jewish ghetto (Via dei Funari 26) recalls an old theatre with a bohemian feel. The grand piano occasionally comes to life during live music evenings. **Fluid** (Via del Governo Vecchio 46; www.fluideventi. com), also near Piazza Navona, is a modern cocktail bar on an otherwise medieval street.

CHILDREN'S ROME

Children love Rome's fountains, the Bocca della Verità (see page 48), the catacombs if they are a bit ghoulish (see page 81) and horse and carriage rides around the city (find them in Piazza di Spagna or in Piazza Madonna di Loreto, off Piazza Venezia). On Piazza Navona there are all sorts of performers and other street-life entertainment.

Children love the city's water features

A favourite with the city's children is the **Villa Borghese park** (see page 57). Here entertainments include pony-rides and a merry-go-round (near Porta Pinciana), bicycle and rollerblade hire (near the Pincio), and a boating lake (near Piazza di Siena). Rome's zoo is also tucked away in a corner and now referred to as **Bioparco** (www.bioparco.it) due to its animal-friendly outlook. Villa Borghese is large and sprawling, so ask for directions or get a map at the tourist office before venturing off.

For the under-12s, the children's museum, **Explora** (tel: 06-3613776, www.mdbr.it, opening hours vary), is at Via Flaminia 82, a 10-minute walk from Piazza del Popolo. Laid out like a small city with a supermarket, a farm, a bank and a water circuit, it's a place where children can touch, observe and play.

And of course there are the numerous *gelaterie*, selling delicious ice cream in multiple flavours; cones begin at about €1.50–2 for one scoop.

FESTIVALS AND EVENTS

1 January New Year's Day. Public holiday.

6 January *Befana* (Epiphany). Festival in Piazza Navona. Public holiday.

17 January Blessing of the animals at Sant'Eusebio, Via Napoleone III.

February/March *Carnevale*. Masked processions and parades.

9 March *Festa di Santa Francesca Romana*. Blessing of cars by the patron saint of motorists, Monastero Oblate di Santa Francesca Romana, Via Teatro di Marcello 32.

March/April Easter weekend. Pope leads the Stations of the Cross *(Via Crucis)* on Good Friday from 9pm onwards at the candlelit Colosseum. On Easter Sunday the Pope blesses the crowds from the balcony of St Peter's at noon. Easter Monday is a public holiday.

April–May Cultural Heritage Week. Free admission to state museums and monuments. *Festa della Primavera*. Spring Festival, azaleas on the Spanish Steps. *Five-day open-air art exhibition in Via* Margutta.

21 April Anniversary of the legendary founding of Rome, celebrated with an evening of fireworks.

25 April Liberation Day. Public holiday.

1 May *Festa del Lavoro*. Labour Day, free rock concert usually held in the square in front of the basilica of San Giovanni in Laterano. Public holiday.

2 June *Republic Day*, with parades on Via dei Fori Imperiali. Public holiday.

29 June *Festa di San Pietro e San Paolo*. Solemn rites in St Peter's Square.

July Festa de' *Noantri*. Two-week long festival in Trastevere with music, food, street theatre, stalls and fireworks.

5 August *Festa della Madonna della Neve* in Santa Maria Maggiore.

15 August *Ferragosto* (Feast of the Assumption). Public holiday.

October Five-day open-air art exhibition in Via Margutta.

1 November *Ognissanti* (All Saints' Day). Public holiday.

2 November All Souls' Day. Romans visit family graves.

December Christmas market and fair on Piazza Navona (until 6 January).

8 December *Festa dell'Immacolata Concezione*. Public holiday.

24–26 December Christmas Eve midnight Mass celebrated by the Pope in St Peter's Basilica. 25 and 26 December are Christmas holidays.

EATING OUT

For Italians, sitting down at the table and enjoying a meal together has always been a celebration. They like to spend hours at the table, chatting with their family and friends and drinking wine. Now that non-residents' traffic has been banned from large sections of Rome's historic centre, outdoor dining can be a delight. The area around Campo de' Fiori (see page 45) and nearby Piazza Navona (see page 41) has become what the Via Veneto was during the days of *la dolce vita* – a place to while away the evening, first at one of the many restaurants and later at an outdoor *caffè*. Other dining spots are Trastevere (see page 72) and the old Jewish Ghetto (see page 47).

WHERE TO EAT

Some hotels, usually the larger ones, serve an English-style breakfast. Otherwise, go to any local bar or caffè and ask for a *caffè* (black espresso coffee) or *cappuccino* (with foaming hot milk), accompanied by a delicious sweet *cornetto* (croissant). Remember that in a bar you will pay at least double if you sit down and are given waiter service instead of consuming any beverages (and food) standing up at the bar *(al banco)*.

For a quick snack at lunchtime, choose a *tavola calda*, a bar with informal tables serving a variety of hot and cold dishes to take away or eat on the spot. Many bars offer the *tramezzino* – half a sandwich on loaf bread containing tuna, chicken or egg

Service included

The restaurant bill will usually include service (called either *servizio* or *coperto*), but ask if you're not sure. It is still customary to leave a small tip.

salad, *prosciutto*, smoked salmon or other ingredients. Or try having sandwiches made at a local delicatessen (*alimentari*). Ask for a *panino ripieno*, a bread roll filled with the ingredients of your choice, which may include sausage, ham, cheese or salad.

In theory, the word *ristorante* usually indicates a larger and more elaborate establishment than a cosier *trattoria* or rustic *osteria*. But in Rome the distinction is often blurred.

Price should not be taken as an indication of the quality of cuisine – an expensive restaurant may offer a superb meal with service to match, but often you pay for the location. Just a few streets off the famous tourist spots such as Piazza del Popolo and Piazza Navona, you'll find *trattorie* with lower prices, more appealing ambience and food with real character. Some restaurants offer fixed-price, three-course meals (*menù turistico* or *prezzo fisso*), which will save money, but you almost always get better food by ordering individual dishes.

Opening Times

Roman restaurants serve lunch 12.30–3pm and dinner 8–11pm. Some offer late-night supper and are open until 1 or even 2am, but on the whole you will be hard pressed to find restaurants serving meals outside the main opening times. They are usually closed one day a week, generally Sunday or Monday. It is

A warming breakfast

better to book by telephone, especially for peak hours (around 1.30pm and 9pm) and peak days (Friday and Saturday). From the middle of August many restaurants close for two to four weeks, as Romans head out of town for their annual holidays.

WHAT TO EAT

Authentic Roman cuisine has its basis in *la cucina povera*, the poor man's cooking. You will find these simple but delicious traditional dishes not only in most Roman *trattorie* but also in the most elegant and expensive restaurants.

Italian happy hour

Come dusk, Romans love to get together for an *aperitivo*, accompanied by a mountainous buffet that often includes all kinds of pasta, salads, cheeses and meats. Most bars in town serve *aperitivo* buffets, but the most copious ones are in the centre, especially in Trastevere and around Piazza Navona.

Antipasti. Any *trattoria* worth its olive oil will have a display of its *antipasti* (hors d'oeuvre) on a table near the entrance. Make your choices and fill your plate. Both attractive and tasty are the cold *peperoni*: red, yellow and green peppers grilled, skinned and marinated in olive oil and garlic. Mushrooms (*funghi*), artichokes (*carciofi*) and fennel (*finocchio*) come cold with an olive oil and salt-and-pepper dressing (*pinzimonio*). A refreshing starter is *mozzarella alla caprese*, slices of soft *mozzarella* cheese and tomato with fresh basil and olive oil. Ham from Parma or San Daniele is paper thin, served with melon (*prosciutto con melone*) or figs (*con fichi*).

Soups. Popular soups are vegetable (*minestrone*), clear soup (*brodo*) and a light version with an egg beaten into it (*stracciatella*).

Pasta. Traditionally served as an introductory course, not the main dish. Even the friendliest of restaurant owners will raise a sad eyebrow if you decide to make a meal out of a plate of

Black pasta with vongole

spaghetti. Besides spaghetti and macaroni try *tagliatelle* or the larger *fettuccine* ribbon noodles; baked *lasagne* with layers of pasta, meat sauce and béchamel; rolled *cannelloni*; and *ravioli*. From there, you launch into *tortellini* and *cappelletti* (variations on *ravioli*), or curved *linguine*, flat *pappardelle*, quill-shaped *penne* and corrugated *rigatoni*. There are almost as many sauces. The most famous, of course, is *bolognese*, or *ragù*. The tastiest version has not only minced beef, tomato and onions but chopped chicken livers, ham, carrots, celery, white wine and nutmeg. Other popular sauces are the simple *pomodoro* (tomato, garlic and basil), *aglio e olio* (garlic, olive oil and chilli), *carbonara* (chopped bacon and egg yolks), *amatriciana* (pork cheek and tomato), *pesto* (basil and garlic ground in olive oil with pine nuts and Parmesan cheese) and *vongole* (clams).

Pizza. Another Italian invention familiar around the world, pizza is in reality a much more elaborate affair than you may be used to; the classic *margherita*, created in 1889 by a Neapolitan chef for Queen Margherita of Savoy, has tomato sauce and melted mozzarella. Toppings can include tomato, ham, anchovies, cheese, mushrooms, peppers, artichoke hearts, zucchini flowers, potatoes, egg, clams, tuna fish, garlic or any other ingredient that takes the cook's fancy. Note that many of the best pizzerias are not open for lunch, as wood-fired ovens take a long time to reach the perfect cooking temperature; say after 8.30 or 9pm. At lunch, Italians tend to buy a slice or two from a vendor, roll it up and eat it standing, or on the street.

Meat. A normal steak served to one person in a US restaurant would feed a family of four in Italy. Portions are smaller, since Italians eat several courses. *Vitello* (veal) is very popular; Rome's speciality is *saltimbocca* (literally 'jump in the mouth'), veal wrapped in parma ham and sage, cooked in Marsala wine. Try the *cotoletta* (pan-fried cutlet in breadcrumbs) or the *scaloppine al limone* (with lemon). *Ossobuco* is a delicious dish of stewed veal shin-bone in butter, with tomatoes, onions, finely chopped lemon rind and marrow. Roman cuisine is also known for the so-called 'quinto quarto', literally the 'fifth' quarter of the butchered animal, meaning its offal. The most typical Roman restaurants will serve *trippa* (tripe), *pajata* (suckling kid or lamb intestines) and *coratella* (heart and lung).

Manzo (beef), *maiale* (pork) and *agnello* (lamb) are usually quite simple: charcoal-grilled or *al forno* (roasted). *Bistecca alla fiorentina* (grilled Florentine T-bone), the emperor of all steaks, costs a royal ransom, but you should try it once.

Romans also claim the best *capretto* (roast kid), *porchetta* (suckling pig, roasted whole on a spit) and *abbacchio* (spring lamb), flavoured with garlic, sage and rosemary and seasoned just before serving with anchovy paste. The most common chicken dishes are *pollo alla diavola* (grilled) or *petti di pollo alla bolognese* (filleted with ham and cheese).

Fish. This is prepared in a simple way – either grilled, steamed or fried. You should look out for *spigola* (sea bass), *rombo* (turbot), *triglia* (red mullet), *pesce spada* (swordfish), *orata* (gilthead), *sogliola* (sole) and *coda di rospo* (angler fish). The *fritto misto* is mixed seafood (fried), consisting of mostly shrimp and octopus.

Vegetables. These are ordered separately, as a *contorno* (side dish); they do not automatically come with the main course. What is available depends on the season, but usually includes *spinaci* (spinach), *cicoria* (chicory), *fagiolini* (string beans in butter and garlic), *piselli* (peas) and *zucchine* (courgettes). Aristocrats among cooked vegetables are the *funghi porcini* (big boletus mushrooms), which are sometimes stuffed (*ripieni*) with bacon, garlic, parsley and cheese. The white truffle is an autumn delicacy and expensive. Try also *peperonata* (red peppers stewed with tomatoes) or *melanzane* (aubergine) sometimes stuffed with anchovies, olives and capers. The Jewish Ghetto originated *carciofi alla giudia* (fried whole artichokes).

Cheese. The famous *parmigiano* (Parmesan), far better than the exported product, is eaten separately, not just grated over soup or pasta. Try also the blue *gorgonzola*, creamy *fontina*, pungent cow's milk *taleggio*, or ewe's milk *pecorino*. *Ricotta* can be sweetened with sugar and cinnamon for a tasty dessert.

Dessert. This often means *gelato*, the creamiest ice cream in the world. It's usually better in an ice-cream parlour (*gelateria*) than in the average *trattoria*. *Zuppa inglese* (literally 'English soup'), the Italian version of trifle, can be anything from a thick and sumptuous mixture of fruit,

Gelaterie abound in Rome

cream, cake and Marsala to a disappointing sickly slice of cake. You may prefer the coffee-flavoured trifle or *tiramisù* (literally 'pick me up'). *Zabaglione* (whipped egg yolks, sugar and Marsala) should be served warm or sent back. *Panna cotta* (cooked cream with a fruit or chocolate topping) and crème

> ### Pasta perfection
>
> There are said to be as many forms of Italian pasta as there are French cheeses – over 400 at the last count, with new ones created every year. Each sauce – tomato, cheese, meat or fish – needs its own noodle.

caramel (an egg custard flan) are also popular staples. Fresh fruit can be a succulent alternative: *fragole* (strawberries), served with whipped cream or lemon, *ananas* (pineapple) and in summer a cool slice of *anguria* (watermelon).

Drinks

Wine. Most restaurants offer the open wine of the house, red or white, in quarter-litre, half-litre or one-litre carafes, as well as a good selection of bottled vintages. Rome's 'local' wine comes from the surrounding province of Lazio. The whites from the Alban Hills are light and pleasant and can be sweet or dry. The most famous is Frascati. From further afield, the Chiantis of Tuscany are available everywhere, as are the velvety Valpolicella from the Veneto and Piedmont's full-bodied Barolo. Look out for the unusual Est! Est! from Montefiascone on Lake Bolsena.

Italian Beer. Beer is tasty but not as strong as north European brands. Peroni, Nastro Azzuro and Moretti are national favourites.

Aperitivo. Campari with soda and lemon is drunk as an appetiser, as is fizzy Prosecco wine from the Veneto region. After dinner, try a glass of aniseed-flavoured *sambuca*. Or go for *grappa*, distilled from grapes, or icy *limoncello*, a lemon liqueur.

TO HELP YOU ORDER...

Waiters are called **cameriere** (men) or **cameriera** (women).
Do you have a set menu? **Avete un menù a prezzo fisso?**
I'd like a/an/some... **Vorrei...**

beer **una birra**
bread **del pane**
butter **del burro**
coffee **un caffè**
fish **del pesce**
fruit **della frutta**
ice cream **un gelato**
meat **della carne**
milk **del latte**

pepper **del pepe**
potatoes **delle patate**
salad **un'insalata**
salt **del sale**
soup **una minestra**
sugar **dello zucchero**
tea **un tè**
water **dell'acqua**
wine **del vino**

MENU READER

aglio garlic
agnello lamb
albicocche apricots
aragosta lobster
arancia orange
bistecca beefsteak
braciola chop
calamari squid
carciofi artichokes
crostacei shellfish
fegato liver
fiche figs
formaggio cheese
frutti di mare seafood
funghi mushrooms
lamponi raspberries
maiale pork

manzo beef
mela apple
melanzane aubergine
merluzzo cod
ostriche oysters
pesca peach
pollo chicken
pomodori tomatoes
prosciutto ham
rognoni kidneys
tacchino turkey
tonno tuna
uovo egg
uva grapes
verdure vegetables
vitello veal
vongole clams

PLACES TO EAT

We have used the following symbols to give an idea of the price of a three-course meal for two, including a bottle of house wine and service:

€€€€	over 70 euros
€€€	45–70 euros
€€	25–45 euros
€	below 25 euros

COLOSSEUM

Luzzi €€ *Via Celimontana 1, tel: 06-7096332*. A very popular neighbourhood trattoria just a short walk away from the Colosseum. Luzzi is loud and cheerful and serves up good pizzas, pasta dishes and simple second courses of fish and meat. The outside tables operate all year round. Lunch and dinner. Closed Wed.

PIAZZA NAVONA AND PANTHEON

Da Baffetto € *Via del Governo Vecchio 114, tel: 06-6861617*. This pizzeria is a rowdy Roman institution, loved by all for the excellent pizza that comes straight from its wood-burning oven. The plain and simple margherita is everyone's favourite and they can't make them fast enough! Credit cards are not accepted. No reservations – just join the queue outside if there is one. Daily 6.30pm–1am; not open for lunch.

Il Convivio Troiani €€€ *Vicolo dei Soldati 31, tel: 06-6869432*, www.il conviviotroiani.com. One of Rome's top restaurants, run by the three amiable Troiani brothers, with Angelo in the kitchen. Imaginative, un-Roman dishes such as quail leg stuffed with foie gras, or minced cuttlefish with roasted peppers. Excellent, fairly priced wine selection. Reservations recommended. Expect to pay about €70 or more per head. Dinner only; closed all day Sun.

Cul de Sac €€ *Piazza di Pasquino 73, tel: 06-68801094,* www.enotecacul desacroma.it. The oldest and one of the best-stocked wine bars in Rome. The space might be tight but the atmosphere and prices are just right. The array of cheeses, cold meats, Middle-Eastern-influenced snacks, hearty soups and salads are of consistently high quality. Be prepared to queue if you arrive at peak times. Lunch and dinner daily; open late.

Da Francesco €€€ *Piazza del Fico 29, tel: 06-6864009;* www.dafrancesco. it. A consistently popular and always buzzing trattoria serving traditional Roman and Italian fare at reasonable prices. The appetiser buffet is particularly rich, and they do crispy, wood-oven baked pizzas at dinner. Open daily for lunch and dinner.

Il Piccolo € *Via del Governo Vecchio 74, tel: 06-68801746.* A lively and casual wine bar that offers a buffet serving a limited selection of traditional fare in a characteristic neighbourhood. Warm dishes are only served at lunchtime; cold platters and salads are on offer in the evening. Eat here before heading to the Piazza Navona for some street theatre. Open daily, lunch and dinner.

La Rosetta €€€€ *Via della Rosetta 8, tel: 06-6861002,* www.larosetta. com. Considered to be the best seafood restaurant in Rome, La Rosetta has next to no meat options. Fillet of sea bass with red wine sauce and artichokes is sublime. Selection of international wines. Reservations essential. Daily noon–11pm.

Terra di Siena € *Piazza Pasquino 77, tel: 06-68307704,* www.ristorante terradisiena.com. A family-run establishment serving traditional dishes from the Tuscan hills. Carnivores will be spoiled for choice here, with a long list of meaty treats, and the 300 plus wine labels include all the Chiantis you can imagine. Mon–Sat lunch and dinner.

Vino e Camino €€ *Piazza dell'Oro 6, tel: 06-68301332.* Italian for 'wine and fireplace', Vino e Camino combines the noble flavour of the best Italian wines with a cosy and warm atmosphere. The food is traditional, "with a touch of creativity", as chef Cristina says. The Sardinian *carasau* bread stuffed with mozzarella and capers, or the tuna fillet skewers with tomatoes and onions are delicious, and the good old pasta *cacio e pepe* is simply perfect. Mon–Sat, dinner only.

CAMPO DE' FIORI AND GHETTO

Ditirambo €€€ *Piazza della Cancelleria 74, tel: 06-6871626; www. ristoranteditirambo.it.* In this rustic and cosy space some imaginative combinations (such as ricotta flan served with sliced artichoke and a fruity pomegranate sauce) are served up to a cheerful and satisfied crowd of tourists and locals alongside traditional well-cooked cuts of meat and fish dishes. The pasta is home-made, as are the mouth-watering sweets. Many options for vegetarians. Lunch and dinner, closed Mon for lunch.

Trattoria Moderna €€ *Vicolo dei Chiodaroli 16, tel: 06-68803423; www. trattoriamodernaroma.com.* Trattoria Moderna has an appealing modern decor of earthy tones. The owners are experienced Roman restaurateurs and the menu is accordingly classical Mediterranean, but with some successful modern touches. Lunch and dinner daily.

Open Baladin € *Via degli Specchi 6, tel: 06-6838989, www.openbaladin. com.* More than 100 Italian artisanal beers and high quality ingredients define this modern restaurant. Order a juicy steak or take your pick from the list of gourmet burgers, which includes the all-Italian buffalo mozzarella cheeseburger. Vegetarians can choose from a selection of salads and first courses. Friendly staff.

Il Pagliaccio €€€€ *Via dei Banchi Vecchi 129, tel: 06-68809595, www. ristoranteilpagliaccio.it.* A highly innovative top-class gourmet experience is to be had in this refined venue. Service is attentive and cordial, and there is an adventurous fixed taster menu. A three course lunch menu costs €75; closed Sun and Mon; Tue open for lunch only.

Trattoria der Pallaro € *Largo del Pallaro 15, tel: 06-68801488; www. trattoriaderpallaro.com.* This quintessentially Roman trattoria is a reliable favourite for big appetites and smaller budgets. There is no menu, but for around €20 (house wine and water included) you will be served several courses one after another and will leave feeling satisfyingly full. The fare is not particularly sophisticated, but is very tasty. The artichokes are excellent and the desserts homemade. The kitchen stays open until past midnight. Lunch and dinner daily. No credit cards.

Piperno €€€ *Via Monte dei Cenci 9, tel: 06-68806629*, www.ristorante piperno.it. Opened in 1856, this long-time favourite in the heart of the Ghetto serves Roman-Jewish specialities, such as *carciofi alla giudia* (fried whole artichokes) and Jerusalem artichokes in a number of delicious variations, as well as fish, veal and pasta dishes. Lunch and dinner; closed Mon all day and Sun for dinner. Reservations recommended.

Al Pompiere €€€ *Via S. Maria de' Calderari 38, tel: 06-6868377;* www.al pompiereroma.com. Waistcoated waiters serve diners in the frescoed rooms of this first floor restaurant located in the picturesque Palazzo Cenci. The dishes are Roman and Roman-Jewish and include some ancient Roman offerings. The standard is consistently good. Lunch and dinner. Closed Sun.

PIAZZA DI SPAGNA AND TRIDENTE

Caffè Canova €€ *Atelier Canova Tadolini, Via del Babuino 150, tel: 06-32110702;* www.canovatadolini.com. In 1818, renowned marble master Antonio Canova turned over his sculpture workshop to his favourite apprentice, Adamo Tadolini, and it remained in the family until 1967. Now it has been transformed into a museum-atelier and full-scale caffè and restaurant, where you can dine all day on small plates amid striking marble creations. Open daily until late.

GiNa €€ *Via San Sebastianello 7/a, tel: 06- 808 8849.* In an almost all-white and funky modern setting, this is a good place to come for lunch, tea, or afternoon drinks. The menu features lots of salads, sandwiches, soups and pasta dishes. Wine is available by the glass or bottle. Dinner daily until 8pm.

'Gusto €€€ *Piazza Augusto Imperatore 9, tel: 06-3226273,* www.gusto. it. 'Gusto has a pizzeria downstairs, an up-market restaurant upstairs, and a wine bar with excellent wines and a great selection of snacks and cheeses on the other side in Via della Frezza. There's also an osteria next to that (at Via della Frezza 16). The quality is always high, service is fast and there is a large porticoed outdoor seating area most of the year round. Lunch and dinner daily.

Nino €€€ *Via Borgognona 11, tel: 06-6795676; www.ristorantenino.it.* Good traditional Tuscan food and Chianti wine selections have been long favoured by the shopowners and patrons of this chic neighbourhood. Nino is reasonably priced for such an expensive area. Try the *taglioni con tartufo nero* (black truffle pasta). Lunch and dinner. Closed Sun.

Obikà €€ *Via dei Prefetti 26/a, tel: 06-6832630, www.obika.it.* Touting itself as the first 'mozzarella bar' in Rome, this minimal chain restaurant pays homage to the delicious cheese that is delivered daily from the neighbouring Campania region. Customers can eat it sushi-style at counters or in a variety of dishes in the elegant restaurant section. There are plenty of options for non-cheese eaters, scrumptious desserts too and a very affordable lunch menu. Lunch and dinner daily.

Rhome €€ *Piazza Augusto Imperatore 42, tel: 06-68301430, www.rhome restaurant.it.* A modern restaurant that strives to make its guests feel at home, as the name implies. Dine inside on luxurious armchairs, or outdoors, in clear view of Augustus' Mausoleum. Mediterranean cuisine and many Roman favourites. Lunch and dinner daily.

VIA VENETO AND TREVI FOUNTAIN

Doney €€€ *Via Veneto 137–141, tel: 06-47082783, www.restaurantdoney. com.* Both the caffè and restaurant lounge attached to the historic Excelsior Hotel are *dolce vita* landmarks and deserve a visit. Constantly renovated and always achingly cool, Doney is the place for a cappuccino by day, an aperitif among the city's cool-conscious crowd, or a dinner of creative and sophisticated Italian cuisine. Open daily from 8am.

Nanà €€ *Via della Panetteria 37, tel: 06-69190750; www.nanaviniecucina. it.* Situated a short walk from Trevi Fountain, this restaurant is a real find in a generally overpriced and low-quality tourist area. The decor is chic and rustic, the staff friendly and the food influenced by southern Italy, with excellent speciality dishes from the Calabria, Sicilia and Puglia regions. Lunch and dinner; closed Mon.

Pane e Salame € *Via di Santa Maria in Via 19, tel: 06-679 1352*. This small, cosy restaurant offers arguably the best sandwiches in Rome, together with excellent cold meat boards and paninis. Be prepared to wait as the place gets crowded. Open daily noon–10pm.

Rinaldi al Quirinale €€€ *Via Parma 11A, tel: 06-47825171*, www.rinaldi alquirinale.it. A very charming restaurant, perfect for a romantic night out. The Roman cuisine offers the best of surf and turf. Top dishes are sautéed mussels, oysters, rock lobster and pasta with porcini mushrooms. Friendly service and more than 300 wine labels. Lunch and dinner daily.

VATICAN AND PRATI

Agata e Romeo €€€€ *Via Carlo Alberto 45, tel: 06-4466115*, www.agatae romeo.it. This restaurant, managed by sommelier Romeo together with his wife Agata (the chef) and their daughter, is considered to be one of the best in Rome. Traditional dishes have a fresh twist and desserts are to die for, including white peach mousse with almond ice cream and dark chocolate fondant with raspberry sauce. Closed Sat dinner, Mon lunch, all day Sun. Reservations essential.

Osteria dell'Angelo € *Via G. Bettolo 24, tel: 06-3729470*. This trattoria serves deliciously hearty Roman dishes at affordable prices. The staff may seem unfriendly at first, but it's part of the show. Mon–Sat lunch and dinner.

L'Arcangelo €€€ *Via G.G. Belli 59–61, tel: 06-3210992;* www.larcangelo. com. The prints on the walls and linen tablecloths form an unexpected backdrop to some very imaginative culinary offerings and an understated gourmet experience. There's a reasonably priced taster menu of Roman cuisine. Lunch and dinner. Closed Sat lunch and Sun.

Bir & Fud € *Via Benedetta 23, tel: 06-5894016;* http://birandfud.it. The odd name is nothing but the Italian phonetic spelling of the English words 'beer' and 'food', and that is exactly what they serve: microbrewery beers on tap and food in the form of delicious pizzas with unusual topping combinations, a number of pasta dishes and homemade desserts. Daily from noon until late.

Checchino dal 1887 €€€ *Via di Monte Testaccio 30, tel: 06-5743816,* www.checchino-dal-1887.com. An acclaimed first-rate trattoria serving traditional cuisine based on the cheap cuts and offal from Testaccio's slaughterhouse. Tripe, brains, liver, sweetbreads and intestines are loved by Romans, but there's much more on offer to keep more conservative palates happy. Lunch and dinner. Closed Sun evening and Mon. Reserve for dinner.

Fish Market € *Vicolo della Luce 2/3, tel: 366 9144 157,* www.fishmarket-roma.com. Invented in Barcelona, the fishmonger-to-restaurant concept is now popular in Rome, too, and it is a great solution for fish lovers who don't want to spend a fortune. Choose the fish from the counter, tell the staff how you would like it cooked, and go get it when it's ready. Fresh fish, loud atmosphere, little service, but very affordable.

Glass Hostaria €€€ *Vicolo del Cinque 58, tel: 06-58335903,* www.glass-restaurant.it. Excellent taster menus, homemade bread and creative dishes such as *tagliolini al nero di seppia con capesante*, *zucchine e pomodorini* (black squid ink pasta with scallops, courgettes and small tomatoes) and *tortelli verdi di trota e ortica con pomodoro fresco* (trout and nettle tortelli served with fresh tomato), make this restaurant in Trastevere a memorable experience. Dinner only. Closed Mon.

Paris €€€ *Piazza San Callisto 7a, tel: 06-5815378,* www.ristoranteparis.it. On offer at this rather un-Parisian restaurant around Termini Station, are a delightful, Baroque dining room and a creative selection of both fish and meat dishes, some highlighting the Jewish side of the city's culinary heritage. In the summer there are a few tables outside in the square. Lunch and dinner. Closed Mon.

Trimani Wine Bar €€ *Via Cernaia 37b, tel: 06-4469630;* www.trimani. com. An excellent choice of wines (the Trimani family first became famous for their nearby wine store) and good food is found in an elegant and friendly atmosphere. Sample a number of good-to-excellent wines by the glass accompanied by a light or full meal at reasonable prices. Open all day; closed Sun.

Ritz Ballroom €€€ *Via V.E. Orlando 3, tel: 06-47092736,.* Sophisticated cuisine in the luxurious dining rooms of the St Regis Grand Hotel. The menu is international, but heavily slanted towards innovative Mediterranean cuisine. Open all day.

FURTHER AFIELD IN ROME

La Pergola at the Rome Cavalieri €€€€ *Via Cadlolo 101, tel: 06-35091,* www.romecavalieri.com. This elegant penthouse restaurant with three Michelin stars has a spectacular view overlooking the city and Roman hills, and an acclaimed chef who creates superb Mediterranean dishes. Reservations essential. Dinner only. Closed Sun and Mon.

Primo al Pigneto €€€ *Via del Pigneto 46, 06-7013827,* www.primoal pigneto.it. This restaurant and wine bar epitomises the edgy hip of Rome's latest gentrification project in the multi-ethnic and young neighbourhood of Pigneto. The menu is a blend of national cuisine and the wine list is hundreds strong. Urban feel and arty crowd. Dinner only. Closed Mon.

A–Z TRAVEL TIPS

A SUMMARY OF PRACTICAL INFORMATION

A

ACCOMMODATION (See also Camping, Youth Hostels and the list of Recommended Hotels, see page 133)

Rome's array of lodgings ranges from the spartan to the palatial. Hotels (*alberghi*) are classified in five categories and graded from one to five stars, based on the amenities and comfort they offer. The Italian Tourist Board no longer uses the term *pensione* in its classifications; these family-style boarding houses are now graded as hotels, usually one or two stars. Some religious institutions also take guests at reasonable rates.

High season is considered to be Christmas, New Year and Easter to October (though many avoid the hot and humid months of July and August). At these times booking ahead is important. For the rest of the year, you can normally find accommodation in your preferred category without difficulty, although decent inexpensive hotels are usually booked far ahead. Rome's official tourist office operates an information website (www.060608.it), an information line (tel: 06-0608) and information kiosks (*punti informativi turistici* or PIT) in various locations around the city (see page 133). All provide up-to-date hotel listings and may be able to help with your booking. Family-run bed and breakfast accommodation can be found at www.bed-and-breakfast.it, while www.cross-pollinate.com and www.airbnb.com list a wide selection of private apartments available for short-term rent.

Room rates should include service and taxes. By law, hotels have to charge an additional tourist tax of €3–7 per person per night. Most hotels have AC; in lower category hotels it may cost extra.

I'd like a single/double room with bath/shower. **Vorrei una camera singola/doppia con bagno/doccia**
What's the rate per night? **Qual è il prezzo per notte?**

Termini station has luggage storage facilities. At Fiumicino, the Hilton Rome Airport is near the main terminal (tel: 06-65258).

AIRPORTS

Rome is served by two airports, Leonardo da Vinci, more commonly referred to as **Fiumicino** (FCO), 30km (18 miles) southwest of the city, and **Ciampino** (CIA), 15km (9 miles) southeast of the city on the Via Appia Nuova (for information on both airports go to www.adr.it, or tel: 06-65951). Fiumicino handles mainly scheduled air traffic; most charter companies and low-cost airlines use Ciampino.

Fiumicino is connected by train to Termini railway station (about every 15–30 minutes; journey 30 minutes; daily 6.23am–11.23pm, from Rome 5.35am–10.35pm); €14; guaranteed on strike days), and to Trastevere railway station (every 15 minutes, on weekends and holidays and after 9pm every 30 minutes; journey 28 minutes; first and last departures 5.21am and 10.21pm; €8). A taxi from Fiumicino to the city centre costs €48; €30 from Ciampino. These fixed fares, set by the authorities, are valid for up to four people with luggage at any time of day or night. A late night Cotral bus runs between Fiumicino and the Tiburtina and Termini train stations when there is no train service. Termini is connected to metro lines A and B, and to buses that go all over the city; Trastevere is linked to the city centre by tram No. 8. There's also the Terravision coach service between Termini train station and Fiumicino and Ciampino airports. Buy tickets online at www.terravision.eu, at the airports' Terravision kiosk or at Termini station's Via Marsala entrance (in front of Terracaffè).

B

BICYCLES AND SCOOTERS

Even though Rome's love affair with public bike system ended with spectacular catastrophe, there are plenty of bike rental companies, including Topbike Rental (Via Labicana 49; www.topbikerental.com), offering all types of bikes. The best day to cycle about is Sunday, when several roads are closed to cars.

For faster and more authentic wheels, check out Bici e Baci scooter rentals (Via del Viminale 5, tel: 06-4828443, www.bicibaci.com). Wearing a helmet is compulsory at all times.

BUDGETING FOR YOUR TRIP

Buses, metro and trains (urban network). Standard fare (*biglietto or BIT*) €1.50 (valid for 100 minutes); one-day ticket (ROMA 24H or *biglietto integrato giornaliero*) €7; two and three-day tickets (ROMA 48H and ROMA 72H) – €12.50 and €18 respectively; weekly ticket (CIS or *carta integrata settimanale*) €24, which allows unlimited travel on all trams, local trains, Cotral buses and the metro for three full days. For timetables, fares and maps, see www.atac.roma.it.

Entertainment. Cinema from €8 to €12, nightclub (entry and first drink) €15–25, outdoor opera €20–80.

Hotels (double room with bath, including tax and service). Prices range from €60 for a one-star hotel (cheaper if it has dorm-beds) near the station to over €1,200 for a suite in a five-star near the Spanish Steps. Almost all hotels lower their prices in the low season so it is worth haggling if you think you're being taken advantage of.

Meals and drinks. Continental breakfast €10, lunch/dinner in a fairly good establishment €20–50, coffee served at a table €2–5, served at the bar €0.80–1.20. Also at the bar: bottle of beer €2–5, soft drinks €2–4, aperitif €3 and up.

Museums. €5–16. Most museums offer free entry once a month (usually on the 1st Sunday of the month), others, namely Musei Capitolini (http://en.museicapitolini.org) are always free.

C

CAMPING

Rome and its environs have some 20 official campsites, most equipped with electricity, water, and toilets. They are listed in the phone directory under *Campeggi, ostelli e villaggi turistici* or on the website www.camping. it. You can also ask in any tourist information point (see page 133) for a full list of sites and rates. A popular campgrounds is Flaminio Village (www.villageflaminio.com), just 6km (4 miles) north of the city centre.

CLIMATE

From June to mid-September, temperatures in Rome range from warm to very hot. It is not unusual to find temperatures above 32°C (90°F) in the afternoon in July and August, when it is best to do major sightseeing in the morning and late afternoon. Winters are cool, often cold, and at times rainy, with occasional snow, but there are many sunny days. Spring and autumn are mild, and the best time to visit.

CLOTHING

Bring light clothing in summer and a rainproof jacket in winter. Bare shoulders and legs must be covered before entering churches, so it is a good idea to always carry a large scarf or a sweater. Very few restaurants have a dress code, but do as the Italians do and avoid shorts when heading to a fancy, high-end establishment.

CRIME AND SAFETY (see also Emergencies)

Pickpockets and purse-snatchers are not uncommon in Rome and tourists are a favourite target. Be careful on crowded public transport (beware the tourist-filled buses 64 and 40 from Termini station to the Vatican, and the metro). Groups of begging children are adept pickpockets, lingering around Termini, the Forum, Largo di Torre Argentina and crowded shopping streets.

> I want to report a theft. **Voglio denunciare un furto.**
> My wallet/handbag/passport/ticket has been stolen. **Mi hanno rubato il portafoglio/la borsa/il passaporto/il biglietto.**

Make photocopies of your airline tickets, driving licence, passport, and other vital documents to facilitate reporting any theft and obtaining replacements. Report thefts to the police, so that you have a statement to file with your insurance claim. The central police station is at Questura Centrale, Via San Vitale 15, tel: 06-46861. For emergencies, call 113.

D

DISABLED TRAVELLERS

Cobbled streets and steep hills are just two of the problems facing travellers with disabilities in Rome. St Peter's, the Vatican Museums, Castel Sant'Angelo, Galleria Doria Pamphili, San Giovanni in Laterano, Galleria Borghese, Galleria Nazionale d'Arte Moderna and a few minor museums are wheelchair accessible. Up-to-date information on access to sights, monuments and hotels is available from Roma Per Tutti (Mon–Fri 9am–5pm; tel: 06-57177094, also English speaking; www.romapertutti.it).

DRIVING

Driving in the city is not advisable, not least because much of the historic centre consists of traffic-restricted zones or pedestrian-only zones, and parking is difficult at best. It is best to get around on foot or by Metro, saving the car for excursions outside the city.

If you need help. Emergency telephone boxes are located at regular intervals on the *autostrade* in case of breakdowns or other difficulties. The **ACI** (Automobile Club of Italy; www.aci.it) runs an efficient breakdown service. If you dial **803116**, you can access their English-speaking operators 24 hours a day.

Driving in Rome. If you must drive in Rome, make sure you check to

I've had a breakdown. **Ho avuto un guasto.**
There's been an accident. **C'è stato un incidente.**

the right and left and your rear-view mirror all the time, and don't take priority for granted with green lights and pedestrian crossings. To progress in a traffic jam, inch gently but confidently forward. Be careful of scooters suddenly passing you on either side.

In the city centre between the river, Piazza del Popolo, Piazza di Spagna, Santa Maria Maggiore and the Colosseum, as well as at night in the San Lorenzo district and across the river in Trastevere, a traffic-restricted *zona a traffico limitato (ztl)* operates Mon–Sat day and night, times vary (for details go to www.060608.it). If in doubt, read the electronic signs at the access of the Limited Traffic Zone: '*varco attivo*' means that access is restricted, '*varco non attivo*' means no restrictions, and you can go. Exceptions to this rule are taxis, buses and cars with permits.

Fuel. Fuel (*benzina*) comes unleaded (*senza piombo or verde*) or as diesel (*gasolio*). Liquid propane gas is marked gpl.

Parking. Parking is one of Rome's greatest challenges. Blue lines designate paid parking areas. Buy a ticket from one of the coin meters. In the centre of Rome the largest and most accessible car parks are: Terminal Gianicolo (www.gianicolo.it) at Piazza Rovere, open 6am–1.30am; Parking Lago Eur (www.apcoa.it) open 24h, on Piazza Terracini; or (the largest, always open) at Villa Borghese (www.sabait.it), entrance at Viale del Galoppatoio 33.

E

ELECTRICITY

Electric current is 220 volts, 50 Hz ac. Bring a multiple adapter plug (*un adattatore*), or buy one as required.

EMBASSIES AND CONSULATES

AUS: Via Antonio Bosio 5, tel: 06-852721, www.italy.embassy.gov.au
Canada: Via Zara 30, tel: 06-854441, www.canadainternational.gc.ca/italy-italie
Ireland: Villa Spada, Via Giacomo Medici 1, tel: 06-5852381, www.dfa.

ie/irish-embassy/italy
NZ: Via Clitunno 44, tel: 06-8537501, www.mfat.govt.nz
South Africa: Via Tanaro 14, tel: 06-852541, http://lnx.sudafrica.it
UK: Via XX Settembre 80a, tel: 06-42200001, www.gov.uk/government/world/italy
US: Via Vittorio Veneto 121, tel: 06-46741, http://italy.usembassy.gov

EMERGENCIES

General Emergency Number (for all services) **112**; State Police **113**; Ambulance **118**; Fire **115**; Road assistance (ACI) **803116**.

> Careful! **Attenzione!**
> Help! **Aiuto!**
> Stop thief! **Al ladro!**

G

GAY AND LESBIAN TRAVELLERS

Rome is less open-minded when it comes to gay and lesbian lifestyle than most other major cities in Western Europe. Openly gay couples are not the norm here, but they are generally tolerated and respected. There are more and more gay and gay-friendly clubs and events, including the Pride parade in June, and the summer festival Gay Village (www.gayvillage.it). The city's 'gay area' is concentrated in and around a gay bar called Coming Out (www.comingout.it), on Via di San Giovanni in Laterano, 8. Associations like Mario Mieli (Via Efeso 2A, tel: 06-5413985, www.mariomieli.org) and ARCIGay (Via Zabaglia 14, tel: 06-64501102, www.arcigayroma.it) provide information.

GETTING THERE (see also Airports)

By air. Rome's Fiumicino (Leonardo da Vinci) Airport is linked by frequent direct service to cities in Europe, North America, the Middle East and Africa. Average flying times are: New York–Rome 8 hours; Los Angeles–Rome 13 hours; London–Rome 2 hours 30 minutes; Sydney–Rome 26 hours.

By car. The Channel Tunnel and Cross-Channel car ferries link the UK with France, Belgium, and Holland. Once on the Continent, you can put your car on a train to Milan (starting points include Boulogne, Paris and Cologne). Alternatively, you can drive from the Channel coast to Rome without leaving a motorway. The main north–south (Milan–Florence–Reggio di Calabria) and east–west (L'Aquila–Civitavecchia) motorways connect with Rome via a huge ring motorway *(grande raccordo anulare)*.

By rail. InterRail cards are valid in Italy, as is the **Eurailpass** for non-European residents (purchase it before you leave home). You can find out more details at www.interrail.eu and www.eurail.com. To buy Inter-Rail passes in the UK go to uk.voyages-sncf.com.

GUIDES AND TOURS

Many private firms offer guided bus tours. A private all-purpose English-speaking travel operation located near the station, **Enjoy Rome** (Via Germanico 8, tel: 06-4451843, www.enjoyrome.com), offers inexpensive walking tours of Rome daily. Several companies offer tours in the open-topped double-decker buses that usually start at Termini station and go past the city's main monuments. Tour operators include **CitySightseeing Roma** (www.roma.city-sightseeing.it), **Big Bus Roma** (http://eng.bigbus tours.com) and **Grayline** (http://graylinerome.com). 48-hour tickets cost about €30 (slightly less in low season). The whole tour usually lasts about two hours and the buses operate between 9am and 5pm. You can hop off and on at any of 8-10 stops on the route.

H

HEALTH AND MEDICAL CARE

EU residents are entitled to the same treatment as Italian citizens but should obtain the European Health Insurance Card, available in the UK from post offices or online at www.ehic.org.uk, entitling them to emergency medical and hospital treatment. To cover all eventualities, travel insurance is recommended. Non-EU visitors should always have private medical insurance. Rome's tap water is not only safe for drinking, but is also considered the best in Italy. Bring an empty bottle when you're out and about, and fill it up at one of the ever-running street fountains.

Pharmacies. The Italian *farmacia* are normally open Mon–Fri 9.30am–12.30, 1pm and 3.30–7.30/8pm, plus Saturday mornings. Usually one operates out of hours in each district on a rotating basis. Its address will be posted in the windows of all pharmacies in the area. Some are open 24-hours, like the Farmacia Internazionale (Piazza Barberini 49, tel: 06-4871195).

> I need a doctor/a dentist. **Ho bisogno di un medico/dentista.**
> Where's the nearest (all-night) chemist? **Dov'è la farmacia (di turno) più vicina?**

L

LANGUAGE

You will not find English spoken everywhere in Rome, as you do in some other European cities. However, Italians are usually helpful and quick to understand what you want. Italians appreciate foreigners making an effort to speak their language, even if it's only a few words. In the major hotels and shops, staff usually speak some English.

Bear in mind the following tips on pronunciation:

'c' is pronounced like 'ch' in change when followed by 'e' or 'i'.

'ch' together sounds like the 'c' in cat.

'g' followed by an 'e' or an 'i' is pronounced like 'j' in jet.

'gh' together sounds like the 'g' in gap.

'gl' together sounds like the 'lli' in million.

'gn' is pronounced like 'ni' in onion.

'sc' + 'i' is pronounced like 'she'.

M

MAPS

The offices of the Rome Tourist Board give away basic street plans; more detailed maps are on sale at newsstands. A free bus, tram and metro network map is available from ticket booths at the Ottaviano and Spagna metro stops on line A. Even more comprehensive public transport maps can be bought from any newsagent and www.atac.roma.it offers a useful journey planner.

MEDIA

A wide selection of English-language newspapers and magazines are on sale at the airport and main railway station, and at newsstands in the centre. The supplement *Trovaroma*, published in the Thursday edition of the newspaper *La Repubblica*, provides listings of cultural events in Rome. Also of interest is the monthly magazine Where Rome, which lists events and shopping and eating possibilities, and is available in many hotels. Another useful English-language publication is the fortnightly Wanted in Rome (www.wantedinrome.com).

The RAI, Italy's state broadcasting system, has three TV channels. There are also various private national and local channels. LA7 offers Fox News broadcasts during the early morning hours (and many hotels offer CNN around the clock). Vatican Radio carries foreign-language religious news programmes. Some radios will tune in to British (BBC), American (VOA) and Canadian (CBC) stations.

MONEY

Currency. Italy's monetary unit is the euro (abbreviated €), which is divided into 100 cents. Banknotes are available in denominations of €500, €200, €100, €50, €20, €10 and €5. There are coins of €2 and €1, and of 50, 20, 10, 5, 2 and 1 cent.

Currency exchange. Currency exchange offices (*cambio*) in the touristy areas are usually open daily 8.30am–7.30pm; some may close on

Sunday. Both *cambio* and banks charge a commission. Banks generally offer higher exchange rates and lower commissions. Passports are sometimes required when changing money.

Travellers' cheques. Travellers' cheques are not accepted everywhere; it is advisable to exchange them at a bank (where you will get better value) at the start of your stay. Passports are required when cashing travellers' cheques.

> I want to change some pounds/dollars. **Desidero cambiare delle sterline/dei dollari.**
>
> Do you accept travellers' cheques? **Accetta i travellers cheques?**
>
> Can I pay with a credit card? **Posso pagare con la carta di credito?**

O

OPENING HOURS

Many offices, larger stores and tourist-orientated shops operate non-stop all day. But much of the city shuts or slows down after lunch.

Shops. Mon–Sat 9am–1pm and 4–8pm (winter 3.30–7.30pm). Half-day closing is usually Monday morning. However, most shops in the centre (Via del Corso, Via Nazionale, Via del Tritone) are open 10am–8pm, and department stores are also open all day. Food stores are open 8.30am–1.30pm and 4–7.30pm (summer until 8pm). Except for supermarkets, there is a half-day closing, usually Thursday afternoon in winter, and Saturday afternoon in summer. Most shops in the city centre or in commercial districts, including supermarkets, now stay open through lunch and on Sunday. Smaller shops and boutiques usually close for at least two weeks between July and mid-September.

Banks. Mon–Fri 8.30am–1.30pm, and again for two hours or so in the afternoon (usually 2.40–4.30pm).

Pharmacies. 8.30am–1pm and 4–8pm (some 24-hours, see page 122).

Churches. Open daily from early morning to noon or 12.30pm, and 4 or 5–7pm. They discourage Sunday morning visits except for those attending Mass. Larger churches and basilicas are open all day.

Museums and historic sites. These are usually open Tue–Sun, 9am–7pm (sometimes earlier), but hours vary.

P

POLICE

The municipal police (*vigili urbani*), dressed in navy blue or summer white uniforms with white helmets, handle city traffic and other city police tasks. Interpreters display a special badge, which indicates the languages they speak.

The *carabinieri*, in dark blue uniforms with a red stripe down their trousers, deal with theft, serious crimes, demonstrations and military affairs. The national, or state, police (*polizia di stato*), distinguished by their navy-blue jackets and light-blue trousers, handle other police and administrative matters. (See also Driving.) The emergency number, 113, will get you police assistance.

> Where's the nearest police station? **Dov'è il posto di polizia più vicino?**

POST OFFICES

Look for the yellow sign with 'PT' in blue. Postage stamps are also sold at tobacconists and at some hotel desks. Post boxes are mostly red – the slot marked *Per la Città* is for local mail only, the one labelled *Altre Destinazioni* is for all other destinations; blue post boxes are for international mail only. For more efficient delivery ask for *posta celere.* It is more expensive, but this way you are guaranteed delivery within three days in Europe and elsewhere in the world. Post offices open Mon–Fri 8.30am–2pm, Sat until 1pm. The main post office, Piazza San Silvestro, is open Mon–Sat 8.20am–7pm. The post office at the station (on Via Giolitti) is open Mon–Fri 8am–7pm, Sat 8am–1.15pm.

> I'd like a stamp for this letter/postcard. **Desidero un francobollo per questa lettera/cartolina.**

PUBLIC HOLIDAYS

Banks, government offices and most shops and museums close on public holidays. When a major holiday falls on a Thursday or a Tuesday, many Italians may make a *ponte* (bridge) to the weekend, meaning that Friday or Monday is taken, too. The most important holidays are:

1 January *Capodanno* New Year's Day
6 January *Epifania* Epiphany
25 April *Festa della Liberazione* Liberation Day
1 May *Primo Maggio* May Day
2 June *Festa della Repubblica* Republic Day
15 August *Ferragosto* Feast of the Assumption
1 November *Ognissanti* All Saints' Day
8 December *Immacolata Concezione* Immaculate Conception
25 December *Natale* Christmas Day
26 December *Santo Stefano* Boxing Day
Moveable date: *Pasquetta* Easter Monday

In addition, Rome has a local holiday on 29 June, the *Festa di San Pietro e San Paolo*, the Feast of St Peter and St Paul, the city's patron saints, when many offices and shops close. Get to St Peter's Square early, as there are huge crowds.

R

RELIGION

Roman Catholic mass is celebrated daily and several times on Sunday. A few Catholic churches have occasional services in English. Confessions are heard in English at St Peter's, Santa Maria Maggiore, San Giovanni in Laterano and San Paolo Fuori le Mura. A number of non-Catholic denominations have services in English. These include: the Church of England at All Saints (www.allsaintsrome.org; Via del Babuino 153B); the Anglican Episcopal church of St Paul's (www.stpaulsrome.it; Via Napoli 58); the Scottish Presbyterian church of St Andrew's (www.presbyterianchurchrome.org; Via XX Settembre 7); and the Methodist church at Piazza Ponte Sant'Angelo (www.methodistchurchrome.com). The Jewish Synagogue is at Lungotevere Cenci 9 (http://jewisheurope.org). The city's Mosque is in Via della Moschea (Parioli).

T

TELEPHONES

Most phone booths around town have been dismantled and public pay phones can now only be found in train stations, airports and schools. These require phone cards (*scheda telefonica*), which cost from €2.50 upwards, while some accept coins or credit cards. Credit-card phones charge very high fees.

Since phone services are expensive in Italy, it may be a good idea to buy an international phone card while staying in Rome. Sold at most newsagents, these cards allow you to call abroad at very low cost using a freephone number. Three of the best ones for the UK and US are called New Columbus, New Welcome and Eurocity, which come in €5 or €10 versions and provide hundreds of minutes.

Those staying for longer periods of time may want to look into getting an Italian SIM for their mobile phone. Please note, your passport or European ID card will be required for registration, so take either with you. The four phone companies (Tim, Vodafone, Wind, Poste Mobile and Tre) constantly change their tariffs, so it's best to compare prices before choosing one.

For Italian directory enquiries, call 1254 or 1240; international enquiries, 892 412, national and international calls via 24-hour operator, 170. Direct dialling for Australia 0061; Canada 001; Ireland 00353; South Africa 0027; UK 0044; US 001.

TIME ZONES

Italy follows Central European Time (GMT + 1). As in the UK, from the last Sunday in March to the last Sunday in October, clocks are put ahead one hour (GMT + 2). The following is a chart of summer times:

New York	London	**Italy**	Jo'burg	Sydney	Auckland
6am	11am	**noon**	noon	8pm	10pm

TIPPING

Though a service charge is added to most restaurant bills, it is customary to leave an additional nominal tip of up to €5 depending on the size of the bill. It is also usual to give porters, doormen, garage attendants and others a little something for their services. As a rough guide, give a hotel porter €1.50 per bag; a chambermaid €3 per day; a lavatory attendant €0.50. Tip hairdressers and tour guides up to five percent. Tipping taxi drivers is optional; €2 will suffice.

TOILETS

Sometimes toilets will be labelled in Italian, but beware: *Uomini* is for men, *Donne* for women; however, *Signori* with a final 'i' is for men, but *Signore* with a final 'e' means women. Some facilities are unisex.

TOURIST INFORMATION

The **Italian National Tourist Board** (*Ente Nazionale Italiano per il*

Turismo, abbreviated ENIT, www.enit.it) is represented in Italy and abroad. They publish detailed brochures with up-to-date information on accommodation, means of transport, general tips and useful addresses for tourists. ENIT has a number of international offices:

Australia and New Zealand: Italian Government Tourist Office, Level 2, 140 William Street, East Sydney NSW 2011, Sydney, Australia, tel: (02) 9357 2561.

Canada: Italian Government Tourist Board, 69 Yonge Street, Suite 1404, Toronto (Ontario) M5E 1K3, tel: (416) 925 4882.

UK and Ireland: Italian State Tourist Board, 1 Princes Street, London W1B 2AY, tel: (020) 7408 1254.

US: Italian Government Tourist Board, 686 Park Avenue, New York, NY 10065, tel: (212) 245 5618; Italian Government Tourist Board, 3800 Division Street, Stone Park,IL 60165, tel: (312) 644-0996, tel: (312) 644 0996/0; Italian Government Tourist Board, Suite 575, 10850 Wilshire Boulevard, Los Angeles, CA 90024, tel: (310) 820 1898.

The Tourist Board in Rome operates an information line (Mon–Sun 9am–9pm tel: 060608) in six languages and a website (www.060608.it) that also lists current exhibitions, concerts, and events. Visit www.turismoroma.it for further, less schematic tourist info.

There are also several useful tourist information points maintained by the city council, which are dotted around the city and open daily from 9.30am–6.30pm. These are at Castel Sant'Angelo–Piazza Pia; Fori Imperiali–Piazza del Tempio della Pace; Piazza delle Cinque Lune (Piazza Navona); Via Giolitti (Stazione Termini); Via dell'Olmata (Santa Maria Maggiore); Via Nazionale (Palazzo delle Esposizioni); Via Minghetti (Fontana di Trevi), Ciampino and Fiumicino airports.

Where's the nearest tourist office? **Dov'è l'ufficio turistico più vicino?**

TRANSPORT

Metropolitana (underground/subway). Rome has two underground railway lines, Line A and Line B. Line A runs from Battistini in the west of the city southeast to Anagnina, stopping at more than 20 stations and passing close to many popular tourist sights (including the Vatican Museums and the Spanish Steps). The intersecting Line B runs from Rebibbia in the northeastern part of the city through Stazione Termini to Laurentina (passing by the Colosseum and the suburb of EUR) in the southwest. The two lines intersect only once, at Stazione Termini. Local trains to Ostia Antica and Lido di Ostia (Rome's closest beach) leave from the station adjacent to the Piramide metro stop (Line B). The metro runs 5.30am–11.30pm (Sat until 12.30am). A third metro line is scheduled to be completed in 2020.

Metro stations are identified by a large red sign with a white letter 'M'. Tickets are sold at newsstands, tobacconists and machines at the metro stations.

Buses and trams. Rome's red, silver and orange buses serve every corner of the city. Although crowded on certain routes and at rush hours, they are an inexpensive way of getting around. Each bus stop (*fermata*) indicates the buses stopping there, their routes, and frequency. Buses run 5.30pm–midnight, after which there is a night service. Tickets for buses must be bought in advance from ATAC booths, some newsstands and tobacconists, or automatic dispensers. There are vending machines on most of the trams. Enter

---

Where's the nearest bus stop/ underground (subway) station? **Dov'è la fermata d'autobus/la stazione della metropolitana più vicina?**

When's the next bus/train to...? **Quando parte il prossimo autobus/treno per...?**

I'd like a ticket to... **Vorrei un biglietto per...**

single (one-way) **andata**

return (round trip) **andata e ritorno**

the bus by the rear or front doors and punch your ticket in the machine; exit by the middle doors; remember that you must ring before your stop. The current bus system is steadily being overhauled, with more ecological and efficient buses replacing the old ones. Trams are mainly used by commuters and connect the city centre with suburbs such as Porta Maggiore or Ostia Antica. Note that ATAC tickets and passes entitle the holder to free travel on urban tram routes only. For visitors, the most useful lines are No. 2 to Piazza del Popolo, Villa Borghese, the Modern Art Gallery and the Olympic Stadium, and No.3, which passes by Circus Maximus, the Colosseum and St. John Lateran.

Tickets. A single ticket is valid for 100 minutes and can be used on as many buses as you wish, but can be used only once on the metro or train. 24-hour tickets (BIG) let you travel as much as you like by train, bus and metro. Weekly tickets (CIS) are sold at the ATAC (transport authority) information booth in Piazza dei Cinquecento, in front of Stazione Termini.

Horse-drawn carriages (*carrozzelle/botticelle*). They can be found at many of the major tourist sites, including the Pantheon, St Peter's Square, the Spanish Steps and the Colosseum. A complete tour around the centre of the city starts at around €80.

Taxis (*tassì or taxi*). Rome's licensed white taxis can be flagged, but it is easier to find them at taxi ranks (in the historic centre two useful ones are located at Largo di Torre Argentina and Piazza Venezia, on the western side of Piazza Madonna di Loreto), or summon them by telephone (tel: 06-6645 or 06-3570). The rates are posted inside.

The meter starts at €3 (€6.50 10pm–6am), and €1.10–1.60 is charged for each kilometre, depending how fast the car is proceeding. There is a surcharge for holidays, Sundays and luggage (the first piece is free, each additional piece costs €1). The law-fixed fare for the journey from/to Fiumicino airport to/from inside the city walls is €48 for up to four people including luggage; €30 to/from Ciampino. Tariffs outside the *gra* (Rome's major ring road) are much higher. Tips are optional. Beware of the non-metered unlicensed taxis (*abusivi*), which are often found at the airport and railway stations.

V

VISAS AND ENTRY REQUIREMENTS

For citizens of the EU, a valid passport or identity card is all that is needed to enter Italy for up to 90 days. Citizens of Australia, Canada, New Zealand and the US require only a valid passport.

For stays of more than 90 days a visa or residence permit is required.

W

WEBSITES

A number of websites provide helpful information for tourists:

www.060608.it The city's official tourist information site with concert and exhibition listings, museum hours and lists of hotels and restaurants.

www.museiincomune.it Useful museum details.

www.enjoyrome.com Useful English-language site.

www.atac.roma.it Public transport.

www.turismoroma.it Official tourist site with useful information for visitors.

Wireless connections can be found in many city-centre caffès. Those travelling without a laptop or smartphone can use the internet in one of the many phone centres/internet caffès found around the Termini and Via Giolitti area.

Y

YOUTH HOSTELS

Youth hostels are open to holders of membership cards issued by the International Youth Hostels Federation, or by the AIG (*Associazione Italiana Alberghi per la Gioventù*). www.aighostels.it, www.hostelworld.com and www.hihostels.com are good resources when planning your trip. Some of Rome's most popular hostels are: Hostel Alessandro (www.hostel salessandro.com); M&J Place (www.mejplacehostel.com); and Pensione Ottaviano (www.pensioneottaviano.com). Beds start at about €18.

RECOMMENDED HOTELS

As a basic guide, we have used the symbols below to indicate high season prices per night for a double room with bath or shower, including service charge, tax and VAT. The hotels listed take major credit cards unless otherwise stated.

€€€€	over €350
€€€	€180–350
€€	€100–180
€	below €70

ROMAN FORUM AND COLOSSEUM

Capo d'Africa €€€ *Via Capo d'Africa 54, 00184, tel: 06-772801*, www.hotel capodafrica.com. A wonderfully peaceful boutique hotel. Behind the dramatic palm tree-lined entrance, Capo d'Africa's 65 rooms are warm yet contemporary in design and feel. The views are delightful, and the Colosseum is only a five-minute walk away.

Edera €€ *Via Angelo Poliziano 75, 00184, tel: 06-70453888*, www.hotel ederaroma.com. This is a quiet, unpretentious hotel with a small garden. Its rates are at the lower end of this price category. No restaurant. Parking spaces available. 51 rooms.

Forum €€€ *Via Tor de' Conti 25, 00184, tel: 06-6792446*, www.hotelforum. comwww.hotelforumrome.com. An elegantly furnished hotel that has a spectacular view of the Imperial Forum from its delightful roof-garden restaurant, a perfect spot for both lunch and dinner. The Colosseum is a very short walk away. 80 rooms.

PIAZZA NAVONA AND PANTHEON

Abruzzi €€€ *Piazza della Rotonda 69, 00186, tel: 06-97841351*, www.hotel abruzzi.it. This is one of the most affordable hotels in the city centre. Unique and dramatic direct views of the Pantheon are its strongest selling point; the 26 rooms are simple but pleasant, and large for Rome. Prices go down in August.

Cesari €€€ *Via di Pietra 89a, 00186, tel: 06-6749701,*www.albergocesari.it. A pleasant, 18th-century hotel, but its past guests – Stendhal, Mazzini and Garibaldi – would not recognise its current look. Very central location. 46 rooms.

Grand Hotel de la Minerve €€€€ *Piazza della Minerva 69, 00186, tel: 06-695201,* www.grandhoteldelaminerve.it. This elegant 17th-century palazzo has provided comfortable lodgings since Napoleonic times. Many of the tasteful contemporary rooms overlook Bernini's Piazza Minerva. Spectacular roof garden. 135 rooms.

Portoghesi €€€ *Via dei Portoghesi 1, 00186, tel: 06-6864231,* www.hotel portoghesiroma.it. A popular, reasonably priced, small hotel in a pic-turesque corner of Rome's Centro Storico. Modern bathrooms, air-conditioning, television and telephones are in each of the 27 comfortable, carpeted rooms.

Raphael €€€€ *Largo Febo 2, 00186, tel: 06-682831,* www.raphaelhotel.com. With a vine-draped façade, this intimate and refined establishment is dec-orated with antiques and works of art in the lobby and in many of the com-fortable rooms. There is both a restaurant and bar in the hotel, but they are easy to overlook with Rome's loveliest piazza (Navona) a few steps away.

Sole Al Pantheon €€€–€€€€ *Piazza della Rotonda 63, 00186, tel: 06-6780441,* www.solealpantheonrome.com. An inn for 500 years, this refurbished boutique hotel retains all its charm while adding modern comforts and enjoying a superb location. Each of the 25 rooms is named after an illustrious guest of the distant past.

CAMPO DE' FIORI AND GHETTO

Arenula €–€€ *Via Santa Maria dei Calderari 47, 00186, tel: 06-6879454,* www.hotelarenula.com. A comfortable, reasonably priced hotel, it's one of the few in the heart of the Jewish Ghetto and is within striking distance of many major sites. 50 rooms. Early booking essential.

Pensione Barrett €€ *Largo di Torre Argentina 47, 00186, tel: 06-6868481,* www.pensionebarrett.com. Though small, with only 20 rooms, this hotel is comfortable and remarkably good value for money. It's also very central and only a five-minute stroll south of the Pantheon. No credit cards. Each rooms is equipped with an expresso machine.

Rinascimento €€€ *Via del Pellegrino 122, 00186, tel: 06-68809556,* www. hotelrinascimento.com. At the lower end of this price category, this pleasant family-run hotel has well-equipped, comfortable and characteristic rooms. Ask for the room with a stunning view of the Chiesa Nuova.

Sole €€ *Via del Biscione 76, 00186, tel: 06-68806873,* www.hotelsole roma.it. One of the few reasonably priced hotels in town, you come here for the delightful terrace and the medieval neighbourhood, alive from early morning until late at night. 58 rooms. Parking spaces available.

PIAZZA DI SPAGNA AND TRIDENTE

Hotel Art €€€–€€€€ *Via Margutta 56, 00187, tel: 06-328711,* www.hotel artrome.com. Located in a former religious college, this hotel successfully blends the old and new. Receptionists greet visitors from futuristic pods in what was once a chapel, with frescoed ceilings, stained-glass windows and a bar where the altar once stood. The 46 rooms are on the small side but colourful and very comfortable. Views are of the arty Via Margutta's terracotta rooftops.

Condotti €€€ *Via Mario de' Fiori 37, 00187, tel: 06-6794661,* www. hotelcondotti.com. A quiet and comfortable hotel, it is in the very heart of Rome's most exclusive shopping district. In this exclusive pedestrian-only area, hotel pickings at relatively affordable prices are slim. 26 rooms.

Gregoriana €€€ *Via Gregoriana 18, 00187, tel: 06-6794269,* www.hotel gregoriana.it. In a very pleasant location at the top of the Spanish

Steps, this converted and renovated convent has a distinctive Art Deco style. Its pretty, comfortable rooms attract regular return guests, many in the fashion industry. 22 rooms and suites.

Hassler Villa Medici €€€€ *Piazza Trinità dei Monti 6, 00187, tel: 06-699340*, www.hotelhasslerroma.com. In a wonderful location overlooking the Spanish Steps and all of Rome, the family-owned Hassler has furnishings, house-proud service and a spectacular rooftop bar to match. A few choice suites have terraces for the absolute splurge. 93 rooms and suites. Wildly expensive but wildly luxurious.

D'Inghilterra €€€€ *Via Bocca di Leone 14, 00187, tel: 06-699811*, www.hoteldinghilterra.com. A perennial favourite sits amid the grid of top-of-the-line designer boutiques near the Spanish Steps. Antique furniture and a fine collection of Neapolitan gouaches preserve a distinct flavour of the past. Celebrity guests such as Ernest Hemingway, Mark Twain and Henry James found it a gem. 88 rooms and suites.

Locarno €€€ *Via della Penna 22, 00186, tel: 06-3610841*, www.hotel locarno.com. A centrally located hotel with an attractive vine-covered façade and art-nouveau interiors. Take breakfast in the lovely small outdoor courtyard, or walk two blocks to the Piazza del Popolo for a sunny alternative. 66 rooms.

De Russie €€€€ *Via del Babuino 9, 00187, tel: 06-328881*, www.roc cofortehotels.com. *The* hotel in Rome. Since it opened in 2000, it has been consistently booked up, and is popular with the stars (George Clooney et al during the filming of *Ocean's Twelve*). Located in Rome's fashionable shopping district, with an atmospheric tiered garden, internal courtyard, and a fitness and spa centre, this hotel gets everything right. Ask for a room with a view of Piazza del Popolo.

Scalinata di Spagna €€€ Piazza *Trinità dei Monti 17, 00187, tel: 06-06-45686150*, www.hotelscalinata.com. The view over the city and down the Spanish Steps from this charming pensione-turned-upmarket boutique hotel is fantastic. The rooms are modest for these rates, but they are always full nonetheless – location, location, location! Wifi access throughout. 16 rooms.

Suisse €€€ *Via Gregoriana 54, 00187, tel: 06-6783649,* www.hotelsuisse rome.com. This is a comfortable, efficient, family-run third-floor hotel in a good location near the Spanish Steps, where some hotels charge quadruple these rates. No fuss and very popular. 12 rooms.

VIA VENETO AND TREVI FOUNTAIN

Aleph €€€€ *Via di San Basilio 15, 00187, tel: 06-422 901,* www.hotelaleph rome.com. In this boutique hotel the 96 bedrooms are inspired by 1930s and 1940s design. A popular top-floor bar and terrace opens in the summer months, and downstairs there is a lovely spa. It was totally renovated in 2016.

Eden €€€€ *Via Ludovisi 49, 00187, tel: 06-478121,* www.dorchester collection.com. This hilltop luxury hotel with beautiful amenities has excellent views of the city from the famous rooftop terrace bar and restaurant. It's halfway between the Spanish Steps and the Via Veneto. 98 rooms underwent full refurbishment at the beginning of 2017.

Excelsior €€€€ *Via Veneto 125, 00187, tel: 06-47081,* www.westinrome.com. The grande dame of the turn-of-the-20th-century hotels is extremely comfortable. It is adjacent to the US Embassy and a natural magnet for Americans and the Hollywood types who fill the sophisticated bar. 316 rooms.

Fontana €€€ *Piazza di Trevi 96, 00187, tel: 06- 6786113,* www.hotelfontana-trevi.com. A comfortable hotel housed in a converted monastery, it has smallish rooms but many of them have priceless views of the Trevi Fountain. Those without a view can retire to the roof garden and terrace. 25 rooms.

Grand Hotel Via Veneto €€€€ *Via Veneto 155, 00187, tel: 06-487881,* www.ghvv.it. Opened in 2009, this five-star boutique hotel is housed inside a grandiose 19th century palazzo; features 116 rooms and deluxe suites, decorated in modern shades of Art Deco and accented with Murano glass. Modern services and timeless style.

ST PETER'S AND THE VATICAN

Atlante Star €€€€ *Via Vitelleschi 34, 00193, tel: 06-6873233,* www. atlantestarhotel.com. Among the attractions offered here is the spectacular 360° view of St Peter's from its well-known and much respected roof-garden restaurant, Les Etoiles, and breathtaking views from many of the 70 rooms. The decor is contemporary and the service courteous.

Columbus €€€ *Via della Conciliazione 33, 00193, tel: 06- 693 45123,* www. hotelcolumbus.net. This tastefully furnished four-star hotel is in a 15th-century palace built by Cardinal (and future Pope) Domenico della Rovere. There are original frescoes in the lobby and a fine restaurant. Three blocks from St Peter's Square, it has been a long-time favourite of visiting Vatican officials. 90 rooms.

Orange €€ *Via Crescenzio 86, 00193, tel: 06-686 8969,* www.orangehotel rome.com. Art Deco meets the 1960s in this boutique hotel where white and orange are the prevailing colours. The gorgeous rooftop terrace offers a breathtaking view of St Peter's. The 28 rooms provide a sensorial experience, with smooth fabrics, aromatherapy and soundproofed windows. Ask for a room with a Jacuzzi.

TRASTEVERE

Hotel Cisterna €€€ *Via della Cisterna 7-8-9, 00153, tel: 06-5817212,* www. hotelcisternarome.com. A short walk from Piazza Santa Maria in Trastevere, this budget hotel has spruced up their simple rooms and adorable inner patio. Exposed brick, terracotta floors, and wood-beamed ceilings and basic furniture offer all necessary comforts. 20 rooms.

Hotel San Francesco €€€ *Via Jacopa de' Settesoli 7, 00153, tel: 06-58300051,* www.hotelsanfrancesco.net. Located in Trastevere, this mid-range boutique hotel exudes old time charm (black and white tiles and baby grand in the lobby) alongside sleek modern design (dark wood and tatame floors in the minimalist rooms), spacious bathrooms and a relaxing rooftop bar with great views. 24 rooms.

Relais Le Clarisse €€€ *Via Cardinale Merry del Val, 20, 00153, tel: 06- 583 34437,* www.leclarissetrastevere.com. This charming hotel dates back to the 12th century and is less than 10 minutes' walk from Santa Maria in Trastevere. The rooms are arranged around an interior garden courtyard and breakfast is served in a former refectory. A great base for exploring the local area, which boasts many restaurants and bars.

Hotel Santa Maria €€€ *Vicolo del Piede 2, 00153, tel: 06-589 4626,* www. hotelsantamariatrastevere.it. This quiet hotel was created around a 16th century cloister, which is now the setting for pleasant outdoor breakfasts or relaxing reads in the sun. The rooms are simple but comfortable, and they all overlook the orange trees in the courtyard. Parking space available.

AROUND TERMINI STATION

The Beehive € *Via Marghera 8, tel: 06-44704553,* www.the-beehive.com. A chic but very cheap option near Termini station, run by an American couple. The Beehive has a dorm room, apartments and private rooms decorated in a colourful and contemporary style, as well as a welcoming garden, a caffè for guests and highly knowledgeable staff.

Britannia €€€ *Via Napoli 64, 00184, tel: 06-4883153,* www.hotelbritannia. it. This comfortable hotel has a refined ambience and a variety of amenities that make the price exceptionally fair. The convenient neighbourhood is safe enough, but not very picturesque. 33 rooms.

Quirinale €€€ *Via Nazionale 7, 00184, tel: 06-4707,*www.hotelquirinale. it. A large, efficiently run and well-decorated hotel just next door to the Teatro dell'Opera, the main reason for its popularity. Outdoor dining in the garden in summer. 209 rooms.

Saint Regis Grand €€€€ *Via Vittorio Emanuele Orlando 3, 00185, tel: 06- 47091,* www.stregisrome.com. Stop by if only for afternoon tea, a year-round tradition, particularly in the winter. Better yet, check into one of Rome's most lavish (and pricey) guest rooms. 161 rooms.

INDEX

ROME

Eighteenth Edition 2017

Editor: Tom Fleming
Author: Patricia Schultz
Head of Production: Rebeka Davies
Picture Editor: Tom Smyth
Cartography Update: Carte
Update Production: AM Services
Photography Credits: Alessandra Santarelli/
Apa Publications 80; Britta Jaschinski/Apa
Publications 85, 86, 93; Fotolia 5T, 78; Getty
Images 5TC; iStock 4TL, 5MC, 18; Leonardo
7R; Ming Tang-Evans/Apa Publications 1, 4TC,
4ML, 5M, 5MC, 5M, 6L, 6R, 7, 11, 12, 15, 24,
26, 29, 31, 33, 34, 37, 39, 40, 43, 45, 44, 49, 50,
53, 55, 57, 61, 62, 65, 67, 69, 70, 73, 75, 76, 83,
100, 102; Shutterstock 4MC; Susan Smart/Apa
Publications 16, 21, 59, 88, 91, 92, 95, 98
Cover Picture: 4Corners Images

Distribution

UK, Ireland and Europe: Apa Publications
(UK) Ltd; sales@insightguides.com
United States and Canada: Ingram Publisher
Services; ips@ingramcontent.com
Australia and New Zealand: Woodslane;
info@woodslane.com.au
Southeast Asia: Apa Publications (SN) Pte;
singaporeoffice@insightguides.com
Hong Kong, Taiwan and China:
Apa Publications (HK) Ltd;
hongkongoffice@insightguides.com
Worldwide: Apa Publications (UK) Ltd;

sales@insightguides.com

**Special Sales, Content Licensing
and CoPublishing**
Insight Guides can be purchased in bulk
quantities at discounted prices. We can
create special editions, personalised jackets
and corporate imprints tailored to your
needs. sales@insightguides.com;
www.insightguides.biz
All Rights Reserved
© 2017 Apa Digital (CH) AG and
Apa Publications (UK) Ltd

Printed in China by CTPS

Contact us
Every effort has been made to provide accurate
information in this publication, but changes are
inevitable. The publisher cannot be responsible
for any resulting loss, inconvenience or injury.
We would appreciate it if readers would call our
attention to any errors or outdated information.
We also welcome your suggestions; please
contact us at: berlitz@apaguide.co.uk
www.insightguides.com/berlitz

Rome Metro / Suburban Rail

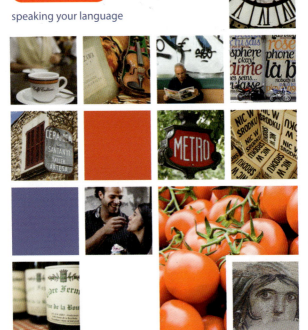

Berlitz®

speaking your language

phrase book & dictionary
phrase book & CD

Available in: Arabic, Brazilian Portuguese*, Burmese*, Cantonese Chinese, Croatian, Czech*, Danish*, Dutch, English, Filipino, Finnish*, French, German, Greek, Hebrew*, Hindi*, Hungarian*, Indonesian, Italian, Japanese, Korean, Latin American Spanish, Malay, Mandarin Chinese, Mexican Spanish, Norwegian, Polish, Portuguese, Romanian*, Russian, Spanish, Swedish, Thai, Turkish, Vietnamese

*Book only